Thermopylae 480 BC

The Most Unequal Battle in History

Thermopylae 480 BC

The Most Unequal Battle in History

DIMITRIS BELEZOS
IOANNIS KOTOULAS

"Come and get them," painting by Christos Giannopoulos.

AUTHORS
Dimitris Belezos - Ioannis Kotoulas

EDITORS (ENGLISH EDITION)
Nikos Giannopoulos, *Historian*
Stelios Demiras

TRANSLATOR
Nikos Th. Tselepides

PROOF EDITOR
Charles Davis

COVER ART
Christos Giannopoulos

**UNIFORM RESEARCH
AND RECONSTRUCTION**
Christos Giannopoulos

ADDITIONAL ILLUSTRATIONS
Romilos Fronimidis
Maria Ginala

ART DIRECTOR AND COVER DESIGN
Dimitra Mitsou

MAPS
Dimitra Mitsou

First published in Greece in 2007
by Periscopio Publications

8, G. Seferi Str., 17234, Dafni, Greece.
E-mail: info@periscopio.gr
www.periscopio.gr

© 2007 Periscopio Publications

ISBN: 978-0-89747-546-4

DIMITRIS BELEZOS

Dimitris Belezos was born in Athens in 1975.
He studied history at the History and Archaeology
Department of the University of Athens and has an
M.A. in Modern Greek History. He has written
various articles related to the ancient and medieval
world for the Greek magazines concerning general
and military history, published by Periscopio
Publications. Four of his monographs, titled
"Crusades," "The Latin Domination Era in
Greece," "Alcibiades" and "The Byzantine Army,"
have also been published by the same publishing
company.

IOANNIS KOTOULAS

Ioannis Kotoulas is a historian and was born in
Sydney, Australia, in 1976. He studied history and
archaeology at the National University of Athens
and has an M.A. in the History of Art. He is
currently writing his dissertation on "Neogothic
Tradition in European Architecture and in Greece"
at the same university. He is the scientific editor
and translator of the series "Historical Archives of
World War II" (Athens, Periplous Publications,
2007). Six of his monographs, titled "Vikings,"
"The Peloponnesian War," "The Army of
Alexander the Great," "Josef Stalin," "The Rise of
the Third Reich," and "Axis War Crimes," have
been published by Periscopio Publications, and
"Intellectuals and Power," was published by
Periplous Publications. Many of his articles have
been published in various historical magazines by
Periscopio Publications and in the Sunday editions
of the newspaper Vima.

Contents

*All the texts have been written by Dimitris Belezos (M.A. in History) with the exception
of "A historical picture of the Battle of Thermopylae," which is the work
of historian Ioannis Kotoulas (M.A. in the History of Art).*

Preface

What was really the essence of the Battle of Thermopylae? Was it a senseless and unnecessary sacrifice? Was it a shining example of extreme devotion to one's own country? Or was it merely a Greek military defeat?

The present volume - faithful to Herodotus's principles for historical accuracy - attempts to provide the reader with answers to the questions above and to present the real dimensions of that almost unbelievable battle.

The Spartans and the rest of the Greeks did not go to the "Gates of Fire" in order to die, but they went for victory! That particular location was, under certain conditions, a position that could be defended by a small but very well-trained military force on the condition that the possibility of outflanking it and encircling it (either from the direction of the coast or from that of the mountain path) could be avoided. This was proven true by the clashes of the first two days (and until the encirclement movement happened), and in essence the opponent's numerical advantage was nullified. The strategic mind and the steel decisions of King Leonidas, the elite Spartan warriors with their incomparable ability to execute complex and dangerous tactical maneuvers in the heat of battle, and the defensive advantages of the position composed a "defense mechanism" capable of repulsing the enemy for an infinite number of times.

As long as the Greek hoplites kept fighting at Thermopylae, the Greek triremes kept defeating the Persian fleet at Artemisium. Although those naval operations were overshadowed by the heroic self-sacrifice of the Spartans and the Thespians, they were in fact of great importance. At Artemisium, the Greek fleet managed to protect the flanks of the Thermopylae defenders. The naval battle of Artemisium was therefore allocated its proper and merited position in this volume as it is integrally connected with the Battle of Thermopylae.

What the Persian rain of arrows, "which hid the sun," did not manage to achieve was ultimately achieved by a mere peasant whose name became synonymous with treason. Leonidas stayed to protect his position although he knew well that on that very same evening he and his warriors "would dine in Hades."

Was it from self-destructive zeal? Was it from respect to the strict laws of the Spartan state, or was it merely an effort to cover the retreat of the rest of the Greek expeditionary forces?
We shall never know the truth.

From a strategic point of view, the fall of the Thermopylae line of defense was a serious defeat for the Greeks. The Persians had achieved their prime objective, i.e., to open a corridor leading to central Greece. This defeat, however, was transformed into an unprecedented moral victory as Leonidas and his 300 warriors became the heroes with which every individual, every community, and every nation and people that must defend their rightful cause at any given moment in history have identified with ever since.

In ancient Greek religion there was little difference between people after their deaths. Everyone ended up in the darkness of Hades and wandered there as former shadows of themselves. There was, however, the possibility for a dead man to enjoy a better fate if he managed to stay alive in the memory of people, if he was seen by the succeeding generations as a symbol and as an example to follow, as was the case indeed for the heroes of the Homeric poems. In order to achieve this fame, however, one had to die in an appropriate manner. It is obvious that the defenders of Thermopylae managed to achieve this distinction.

Nikos Giannopoulos
Editor

A limited glossary has been provided at the end of this book that covers most of the terms that the readers may be unfamiliar with. It is in alphabetical order for ease of use.

The preparations of the opposing forces
The events leading up to the epic battle

Well before the time of Xerxes' invasion of Greece, Persia had revealed, in a number of ways, its aggressive intent against the free Greek cities of the Western Aegean. The events leading up to the invasion and the opposing forces' preparations for the titanic struggle that would follow were a decisive factor in the developments that ultimately led to the Battle of Thermopylae.

By the beginning of the 5th Century BC, the Persian Empire had expanded into the heart of the Greek world.

They had occupied the kingdom of Lydia in 546 BC. Lydia then went on to subjugate the Greek cities of Ionia in the first half of the 6th century BC. The region included some of the wealthiest and most cultured Greek cities.

The most important city among these was Miletus, as it was a great commercial and cultural center and the metropolis for many of the colonies in the Mediterranean and the

A feline god from the palace of Darius I at Susa.

Black Sea. Equally powerful and wealthy was the city of Ephesus, one of the most famous and beautiful cities of antiquity. These Ionian cities were considered the center of Greek civilization. They had indeed become enormously affluent from their commercial activities and were also important cultural centers for philosophy and Greek scientific thought that was later to form the basis of European civilization. The conquest of these cities, first by the Lydians and then by the Persians, meant that a significant part of Hellenism - the wealthiest and most culturally advanced - found itself under foreign rule. The Lydian occupation was not very oppressive as their king, Croesus, thought highly of the Greeks. He was closely attached to the Oracle of Delphi, respected and often honored it, and foremost Greek thinkers, such as Solon, were always among his guests.

Following the downfall of the Lydian kingdom that preceded the dominance of the Persians, the plight of the Ionian Greeks worsened. They were now subjugated to a dynastic ruler, who resided at a great distance and did not hold their civilization in any particular esteem. To the Persians, the Ionian Greeks were merely taxable subjects, like all others in their empire. The Persians placed tyrannical rulers in charge of the Greek cities, as they believed that it would be easier to control tyrants than to cooperate with a democratic or an oligarchic form of government. The Persian satrap, who normally resided at Sardis,

The location of Xerxes' canal that was cut to avoid having to sail around the cape of Mt. Athos.

An illustration of a gold Persian sword (akinakes) used for traditional ceremonies. (illustration by Romilos Fronimidis)

Tombs of Persian kings at Naghsh-e-Rustam.

A bronze statuette of a hoplite from the Museum of Dodoni.

was responsible for the supervision of the Greek cities of Ionia and held sway over all of Asia Minor.

For the Persians, however, it soon became apparent that it would be difficult to control the Greek regions skirting the eastern coast of the Aegean, as there were other, free Greek city-states close by. To that end, they had conquered the Greeks living on the islands of the Eastern Aegean. However, they were well aware that their presence in the region would not remain secure for long, as the other free Greek cities along the

Aegean's western coast were just a few days sailing from Ionia.

The Persians' fears were confirmed in 499 BC when the Ionians revolted, after the Ionian cities had been persuaded by Miletus' tyrant, Aristagoras, to rise up against their Persian overlords. The Ionian Greeks sent a request to the Greeks on the other side of the Aegean for support in their conflict against the Persians. The cities of Athens and Eretria, whose citizens belonged to the Ionian race (incidentally, so did most of the Greeks of Asia Minor!), sent a small expeditionary force in the form of a small fleet consisting of 20 Athenian and five Eretrian triremes. The Ionian revolt failed, however, with the Ionian Greeks being defeated at the naval Battle of Lade, followed by the retaking of Miletus and with the city put to pillage. The Persians wanted to capture and punish any who had assisted the rebels.

In 492 BC, just a few years after the suppression of the Ionian revolt, a Persian fleet, led by Mardonius, attempted the invasion of Greece by sailing along the coast of Macedonia. Fortunately, the fleet was hit by a storm off Mount Athos, on the Chalcidice Peninsula, and most of the force perished. Moreover, this naval disaster had the additional effect of making the Persians doubly cautious in their future conduct of naval operations in the Aegean. Two years later, in 490 BC, yet another Persian fleet, led by two generals, Datis and Artaphernes, crossed the Aegean and sailed, via the Cyclades Islands, directly to Euboea. It then laid waste Eretria, thus punishing its people for the help they had provided during the Ionian revolt. From there, the Persians sailed toward Attica, landing at Marathon. Upon landing, they were confronted by a small force of Athenians and Plataeans, under the leadership of Miltiades, and suffered a humiliating defeat at the famous battle of Marathon.

Xerxes is incited to invade Greece

The Marathon defeat did not discourage King Darius but made him realize that war with the Greeks would be a difficult undertaking and would require long-term and better preparations. Darius spent three years assembling his armies and building ships in order to launch his next attack. During the fourth year of these preparations, however, Egypt revolted and the Persian king was forced to

turn his attention to that region. Unfortunately, he did not manage to send a force to Egypt in time, as he died a few months later. His son Xerxes, the "Great King," succeeded him and he immediately decided to continue the work of his father. The subjugation of Egypt was a high priority, as that region was a Persian province. After a short military campaign, Egypt was reconquered and was placed under a new, tougher, and more oppressive form of rule. As soon as the Egyptian military expedition was completed, Xerxes began to prepare for his offensive against Greece. Mardonius, his cousin, was instrumental in inciting him to attack the Greeks, as he reminded him of the humiliation his kingdom had

The head of a Persian bull or sacred cow (gauw) at the Palace of Persepolis.

The "hunters' amphora." Hunting was a Spartan's favorite pastime, also of many of the ancient Greeks, as it was considered a type of military training. (Archeological Museum of Sparta)

suffered at the hands of the Athenians, who had helped his subjects to revolt, and still remained unpunished. Mardonius even made the point that it was illogical for Persia to hold people who had never caused trouble under Persian rule while allowing the Greeks, who had supported the Ionian revolt, to remain free. Mardonius also talked of the wealth of Europe, and argued that these riches should fittingly belong to the Persian "King of Kings." Mardonius' argument proves that the Persians never intended to halt their expansion in Greece but always wanted to advance further west. It appears that the Persians were aware that Greece was not particularly rich, and could not therefore offer them a large amount of income from taxation and other riches. Its occupation seemed desirable for two main reasons: first, to assure the constant subjugation of the Greek cities of Ionia, and second, to give the Persians a forward base from which to expand into the western Mediterranean.

Apart from Mardonius, certain Greeks incited Xerxes' to undertake a military expedition against Greece. The Aleuad family was one of the most powerful family clans in Thessaly, and many of its members had served as tagoi, i.e., leaders of the community federation (koinon) of Thessaly. Since their authority in Thessaly was constantly doubted, they tried by all means to secure their power with the support of the Persians. The Aleuads had summoned the help of an oracle, Onomacritus, the famous Greek reader of omens, who visited the Persian Royal Court and divined that Xerxes was destined to join the two coasts of the Hellespont and to invade Greece. Onomacritus, who had been paid to persuade Xerxes to launch his invasion soon, did not prophesy any possible defeat, but restricted himself to expounding only on the glory and the profits that were in store for the great conqueror. Xerxes received similar persuasion from the Peisistratids, the descendants of

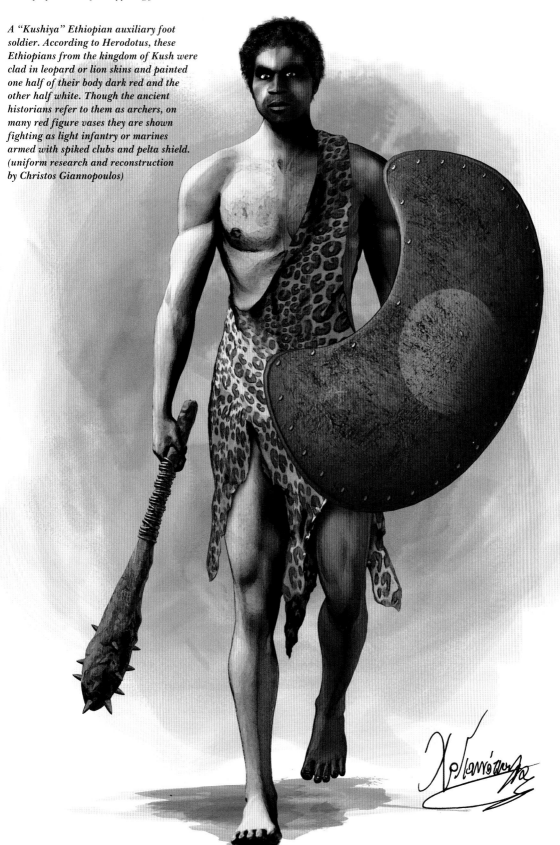

A "Kushiya" Ethiopian auxiliary foot soldier. According to Herodotus, these Ethiopians from the kingdom of Kush were clad in leopard or lion skins and painted one half of their body dark red and the other half white. Though the ancient historians refer to them as archers, on many red figure vases they are shown fighting as light infantry or marines armed with spiked clubs and pelta shield. (uniform research and reconstruction by Christos Giannopoulos)

A painting on enamel-coated brickwork from Susa. Two winged lion gods with a proto-Zoroastrian symbol hovering overhead. In the inset, the name of Xerxes I (486-465 BC).

Peisistratus, the former tyrant of Athens. Hippias, the son of Peisistratus, who had succeeded his father as tyrant of Athens, had been overthrown and chased from the city, finding shelter in the Royal Court of Persia. When the Persians landed at Marathon at 490 BC, Hippias accompanied them, hoping that they would reinstate him as tyrant of Athens. His supporters had tried to cooperate with the Persians at the time and had attempted to betray their city. Despite the defeat at Marathon, his relatives continued to believe that one day they would return to power in their home city with the help of the Persians.

Another, more important fugitive from Greece also lived in the Persian king's Court. This was the former king of Sparta, Demaratus, who had lost his throne when his official family lineage had been placed in doubt. Demaratus had initially been advisor to Darius and, later, also to Xerxes and hoped he would be able to return to Sparta with Persian support. Many claimed at the time that Xerxes owed his throne to Demaratus and, because of that debt, Xerxes held him in esteem and great respect. Darius had many sons, and Xerxes was not the first-born. According to Herodotus, when Darius was trying to decide if he should appoint his first-born son or another son as his successor, Demaratus had explained the succession law existing in Sparta. According to Spartan law, the king was to be succeeded not by the first-born son but by the first son to be born after the father had been enthroned. Darius judged this legal custom as more correct than succession based on the first-born principle, so he decided to appoint Xerxes as the successor to the throne instead of his elder brother.

The decision to invade

Xerxes held a council with his closest relatives and the empire's highest-ranking officials before beginning preparations for the invasion. During the course of the council, he announced his decision to invade Greece. Mardonius immediately showed approval of the king's decision and convinced the council members that victory was assured.

According to him, the Greeks in many city-states were divided and clashed with each other and would be unable to unite to face the enemy assault. He also claimed that the fighting tactics of the Greeks were inferior to those of the Persians.

Artavanus, one of Xerxes' oldest uncles and Darius' brother, disagreed, reminding everyone that the Persians had already suffered one defeat at Marathon and, therefore, the battle tactics of the Greeks were not, it appeared, at all inferior to those of the Persians. He was also worried about Xerxes' plan to build a bridge across the Hellespont and then cross it with a large army. If the Greeks managed to destroy that bridge, Xerxes and his army would be trapped on European soil, while the Asians would make good use of the opportunity and

revolt. Artavanus even mentioned a similar expedition undertaken by Darius in the past, when Xerxes' father had crossed the Bosphorus Straits and advanced through Thrace to the banks of the Danube. He had then built a bridge and invaded Scythian territory to subjugate it. However, while the Persian army still lay encamped on Scythian territory, far from the Danube bridge passage, the Scythians asked the bridge guardians to destroy it and thus trap the Persians. The bridge guardians were Ionian Greeks from various city-states that were under the rule of tyrants imposed by the Persians. Despite the fact that these tyrants had gained power through Persian support, they were tempted by the Scythian request, as they envisaged an opportunity to free themselves of Persian domination and retain their power without having to justify their actions to any superior authority. In the end, they did not destroy the bridge, mainly because Histiaeus, the tyrant of Melitus, dissuaded them. However, according to Artavanus, it had been a mistake to have the King of Persia and his kingdom's future dependent on the good will and abilities of a foreigner. Also, Xerxes could not afford to place his kingdom at risk for a second time. Artavanus' words did not change Xerxes' mind to attack Greece. It is possible that Artavanus' opposition to the plan may not be based on fact, as it could be imaginative fiction inserted by Herodotus in his narrative. Herodotus may have added this fictional dimension to his Greek history of the Persian Wars in an effort to make his narrative more balanced, presenting Xerxes as wavering between the two opposing views, the one urging him to start a risky war and the other to make him seek a safe peace. It is

A relief sculpture from Persepolis depicting a Persian "Immortal."

The ruins of ancient Sparta.

specific locations within the Persian Empire where provisions for the army were to be stored were also now determined. The king's representatives were charged with the selection of these locations so that they lay in areas suitable for the most efficient maintenance of the provisions. In this way an extended chain of replenishing areas for the Persian army was created stretching from the heart of Persia to the borders of Macedonia. The invasion had not yet begun, yet thousands of people were already involved in the gathering of provisions and the creation of logistical support bases.

The preparations, however, were not limited to the conscription of troops and the gathering of provisions. As Xerxes did not want to suffer a disaster similar to that of 492 BC off Mt. Athos, he ordered the digging of a canal across the northern part of the Chalcidice Peninsula. In order to cut the canal, he sent ships to the area under the leadership of Megabazus' son, Bubares, and Artaeus' son, Artachaees. The natives of Athos were forced to help in the construction of the canal. In company with workers who had been brought from various regions of the Persian Empire, these locals worked hard under the threat of Persian punishment by whip-wielding overseers. According to Herodotus, this undertaking was of both practical and psychological value. By constructing the canal, the "Great King" believed that it would demonstrate his power to the Greeks and force them to think twice about any form of resistance. When the canal construction at Mt. Athos was completed, after almost three years, the same laborers were then used to build bridges across the Strymon River for the passage of the Persian army. The Kingdom of Macedonia, to which

also equally possible that there were real arguments against Xerxes' plan on the part of some of his advisors, although it remains doubtful that Artavanus was one of them.

Preparatory Persian operations

Xerxes' preparations for the assault on Greece took four years following the suppression of the Egyptian revolt. Each province of the Persian Empire was given the task of assembling and training a specific number of troops and collecting the required provisions. The Phoenician and Ionian Greek coastal cities were ordered to prepare ships and train their crews. The

this area belonged, was forced to put up with the Persian activities as it was, at that time, subjugated to the Persians. This was due to the failure of Mardonius' previous invasion. His expedition of 492 BC had not managed to reach Attica, but had only been able to impose Persian rule along the northern coastal regions of the Aegean Sea.

Once the invasion route was ready, Xerxes began the task of assembling his army. He had designated Sardis, the old capital of the Kingdom of Lydia and the seat of the satrap of Asia Minor, as the initial assembly point for his troops. The Persian king joined the Persian infantry at Kritalla in Cappadocia, and advanced on Sardis from there. While Xerxes remained at Sardis waiting for his armies to gather, he sent messengers to the Greek city-states requesting water and earth as a sign of submission. The Persians had acted similarly during the previous invasion that had culminated in the Battle of Marathon. According to Persian doctrine, cities that had declared themselves subjugated were considered a part of the Persian Empire and were obliged to confirm it by action. Xerxes was certain that the cities that had previously refused to offer water and earth would succumb through fear as soon as they heard of the size of the Persian army. He did not, however, send any messengers to Sparta or Athens as, years earlier, the inhabitants of those cities had killed those that had been sent for the same reason. The Athenians had thrown them into a deep crevice, while the Spartans had dropped them into a water well and told them to get water and earth from there. Xerxes attempted to terrorize the Greeks even further by using captured Greek spies who had been sent to observe the Persian army camp at Sardis and

report on the number of the troops. These spies had been captured, ordered to be tortured and then to be executed. However, when Xerxes learned of this, he immediately rescinded the order and freed them and paraded them throughout his camp. He believed that once the spies returned to their Greek homelands, they would spread the news that an incredible army of enormous size was preparing to invade and that this would undermine the will of the Greeks to resist.

The Hellespont bridge

While the Persian army was gathering at Sardis, Xerxes ordered the beginning of the construction of the bridge over the Hellespont, the most important and impressive undertaking for the support of the invasion. The location of the proposed bridge was to be at the point where the European coast ended in a promontory with the land jutting out farthest toward the Asian land mass. This promontory was situated between the cities of Sestos and Madytos, while on the opposite coast lay the city of Avydos. At that time, the distance between the two

A bust of Herodotus, the historian who, in his writings, describes the Greco-Persian wars in detail. (a contemporary copy from the War Museum of Athens)

These votive offerings from Spartan temples were gifts from poor visitors and were made of lead. They mainly depict warriors, but could also include gods and hunters. (Archeological Museum of Sparta)

coasts must have been smaller than it is today because the sea currents have widened the straits during the intervening centuries. The Persians thus began construction of two bridges from the Asian side of the strait, at a location near the city of Avydos, extending the bridges out to sea toward the promontory on the opposite shore. The construction was in the form of pontoon bridges made of boats tied together with thick ropes upon which a plank gangway was to be attached from boat to boat, thus forming a wooden road over which the army could pass to the European coast. The construction of one of the two bridges had been placed in the hands of the Phoenicians, who were in the habit of using white linen ropes. The second bridge, meanwhile, was to be constructed by the Egyptians, whose custom was to tie the boats together with papyrus ropes. The work progressed rapidly, and was near completion when a sudden, severe storm broke and destroyed the bridges. Xerxes was so angry that he tried to prove his power over the sea. He ordered that the waters of the Hellespont be given 300 lashes while, simultaneously, the following words were spoken to the waters of the sea "Bitter Water, the King is giving you

A Phrygian sword-bearing peltast (takabara). The Thracians of Asia, who lived in the hilly regions of western Anatolia (Phrygians, Armenians, Cappadocians, Cilicians, Bithynians, etc.), were used as auxiliary infantry and often as an auxiliary marine force. The Phrygian warrior in the illustration is equipped in the usual fashion of his nation: a leather hat with side wings, a long mantle, garments decorated with geometrical patterns, leather greaves, a pelt-type shield (taka in Persian). He also carries javelins and grasps an Iranian-style curved, slashing sword. (uniform research and reconstruction by Christos Giannopoulos)

The Persian army crossing the Hellespont bridge. (C.M. Bowra, Classical Greece, "Time Life", 1965)

this punishment because you have shown yourself unfair while he has never offended you. King Xerxes will cross your waters whether you like it or not. That no man ever offers sacrifice in your honor appears justifiable as you are merely a salty and murky river." The Persian monarch went so far as to order the Hellespont be burned with a hot iron that was symbolically immersed in the water. The burning of one's back with a hot iron was the customary punishment for slaves who had escaped. The Persians also threw a pair of chains into the sea to secure the subjugation of the Hellespont. This gesture, however silly and exaggerated it may now seem to us, had a symbolic and special significance for the Persians and their conquered peoples. It was proof that their king was so strong that

he had the power to subjugate the natural elements. Xerxes also punished the men in charge of the construction and had them beheaded. The significance of Xerxes' behavior was entirely different for the Greeks. To them, the whipping of the sea was an unreasonable excess and constituted proof of unwarranted pride that prevented man from staying within human limitations. According to Greek belief, the Gods punished such arrogant pride.

Those who now took charge of the reconstruction of the bridges went to great lengths to build them stronger and more durable than before, and to make good use of the currents that dominated the waters of the strait. For the northern bridge, they utilized 360 ships, triremes and pentaremes, for support, with another 314 ships for the southern bridge. The bridges were so constructed that the current passing at that point held the holding ropes taut. Heavy anchors were also dropped into the sea to maintain the ships in position. These anchors were dropped on the windward side of each bridge so as to better withstand the wind pressure. Three small open passageways were also left in each bridge so that ships sailing to and from the Black Sea could pass through the strait unhindered. The bridge builders were also careful to keep the ropes holding the bridges to the coast taut. Instead of using different types of rope for each bridge, a combination of the two types of ropes were used so that each bridge was held in place by two white linen ropes and four papyrus ropes. When the connection between the two coasts was established, many uniformly cut tree trunks were placed on the ends of the taut ropes in order to form a foundation for the pathway across the top of the bridge. A solid decking of wooden criss-crossing planks was then placed on these trunks. This decking was then covered with a layer of compressed earth to form a roadway across which the army could march. Wooden walls were also erected on each side of the roadway so that seeing the water from such a height would not frighten the animals crossing the bridge. Finally, large moles were constructed at the bridge's junction points and the land, so that the movement of soldiery and animals would be further facilitated.

The Persians cross into Europe

When the construction of the Hellespont Bridge and the Mt. Athos Canal were finally completed, the Persian army stood ready at Sardis. With spring nearing, Xerxes ordered the march toward the Hellespont to begin. To assure himself of the success of his expedition, the Persian king resorted to a barbarous custom.

A lion painting on a Corinthian amphora, 575 BC.
(Museum of Corinth)

According to Persian beliefs, a bad turn of events could be avoided if an animal were sacrificed by being cut in half and having the army march between the two pieces. To that end, Xerxes ordered the son of a Lydian leader, who had previously insulted him by doubting the successful outcome of his invasion, be cut in two. The two parts of the victim's body were then erected on each side of the road his army would take, so that the soldiers would pass between them.

During the march to the Hellespont, the men carrying utensils and stores and the animal-drawn carts were in the lead with the remainder of the army following. The troops did not march in groups of distinct units or nationalities but proceeded in mixed order. Xerxes and his entourage were in the middle of his army, with about a half-kilometer separating them from the troops in the front and rear. Leading the Xerxes' section were 1,000 Persian elite cavalrymen. Behind them came the ten sacred horses, followed by the sacred chariot of the Persians' most important deity, their god Ahura Mazdah. Next came Xerxes' chariot. When the king felt tired, he retired inside a luxurious covered chariot. Xerxes' chariot was followed by elite lancers and another 1,000 elite Persian cavalrymen. The cavalry was followed by the 10,000 so-called "Immortal" infantry. Bringing up the rear of the royal procession were 10,000 Persian cavalry. All the men in Xerxes' entourage were lavishly dressed and their lances had gold or silver bases in the form of apples and pomegranates. A large part of the provisioning and logistical support troops at the head of the army catered to the needs of the royal entourage. Even the Great King's lowest-ranking bodyguard was resplendent in a uniform covered in gold and silver ornamentation, while the elite part of the bodyguards, the 10,000 "Immortals," were accompanied by their concubines. Their provisions were carried on the backs of special camels, separate from the food of the rest of the army.

The Persian army marched up through the western regions of Asia Minor and arrived at Avydos, on the Asian coast of the Hellespont. The residents of that city had erected a marble platform from where Xerxes could survey his army and fleet. To provide amusement for the king, while at the same time train the fleet, sea races were organized. The winners were the Phoenicians from the city of Sidon. The following day, the army crossed the pontoon bridges onto European soil. An interesting detail was that, as soon as the sun rose, Xerxes offered votive deposits to the sea by dropping wine from a golden cup into the water. This was followed by the cup itself, then a second golden crater cup, and, finally, a Persian sword. Only then did the army start to cross. The infantry and the cavalry used the northern bridge, nearest the Hellespont side. The men who carried the provisions, and the servants used the southern bridge, nearer the Aegean side. Xerxes, with his entourage and his cavalry, crossed into Europe the following day. Herodotus states that seven days and nights were required for the whole army to cross to the other side, a comment that today appears grossly exaggerated.

The Persians in Thrace and Macedonia

The army marched westward from the bridges and arrived at Doriskos, near the mouth of the Evros River. At

this point, Xerxes decided to count his army. Herodotus writes that a circle, in which 10,000 could stand, was drawn on the ground and then the army entered the circle in sections so that a rough estimate of its size could be calculated. According to Herodotus, Xerxes' land forces consisted of 1,700,000 troops. Following the counting, the soldiers were grouped by nationalities. The largest nationality was, of course, the Persians, commanded by Otanes, the king's father-in-law. The Medes, commanded by Tigranes, came second, then came the Kissians, commanded by Anaphes, the son of Otanes and brother of Xerxes' wife. The Assyrians were led by Otaspes. All these races were familiar to the Greeks, but the Persian army also included certain peoples who were still foreign to the residents of the Mediterranean coasts. Among them were the Bactrians and the Sacans, who lived on the Persian Empire's eastern borders and who were led by Xerxes' brother Hystaspes. The Indians were commanded by Pharnazathres and the Arians by

The ruins of ancient Corinth, where the Greeks held their Council to decide how best to oppose the Persian invasion.

Sisamnes. The Parthians and the Chorasmians, commanded by Artabazos, came far from the east. There were also the Sogdians, led by Azanes, the Gandarians, and the Dadicans, commanded by Artyphios. Ariomandros, the brother of Artyphios, commanded the Caspians.

Persian army ranks also included the Sarangians, led by Pherendatis, the Pactyans under Artayntes, the Utians and the Mycans under Xerxes' brother, Arsamenes, and the Paricanians under Siromitres. From the southern and the eastern regions of the Persian Empire came the Arabs and the Ethiopians led by another of Xerxes' brothers, Arsames, and the Libyans under Masagges. From the empire's western regions came the Paphlagonians and the Matienians, the latter led by Dotos, the Mariandynoi, the Lygians, and the Syrians commanded by yet another of Xerxes' brothers, Gobryas.

From the central and eastern regions of Asia Minor came the Phrygians and the Armenians, commanded by Artochmes, who was married to one of Xerxes' sisters. From western Asia Minor came the forces of the Lydians and the Mysians, commanded by Artaphenres, the son of the Artaphenres, who, together with Datis, had invaded Marathon and had been defeated.

Contingents from many smaller nations followed, under the command of famous Persian generals, some of whom were the king's close relatives. The whole of the infantry was under the command of Xerxes' two cousins, Mardonius, son of Gobryas, and Tritantaichmes, together with Smerdomenes and Masistes, the younger brother of the Persian king, and Megabyzos. The cavalry commanders were Harmamithras and Tithaios, sons of the same Datis who

had been one of the two Persian commanders at the battle of Marathon. Finally, the 10,000 "Immortals" were commanded by General Hydarnes.

The size of the Persian fleet was analogous to that of the army, and its composition was also multinational. Various estimates of the size of the fleet have been published and many seem exaggerated. According to the text in Aeschylus' tragedy "The Persians" and also to Herodotus, the Persians possessed 1,207 vessels, of which 207 had a speed and maneuverability similar to that of the Greek ships. This estimate appears to be closest to the truth. Herodotus also mentions an additional 3,000 smaller vessels, most with 30 to 50 oars, and other auxiliary vessels (kerkouroi) for transporting troops, horses and provisions. He also refers to an additional 850 horse-carrying vessels. These vessels required more than 50,000 sailors, oarsmen and soldiers to operate and, if one also adds the men required for auxiliary tasks, the total of those serving in the Persian fleet, according to Herodotus, rises to one million men. That figure also appears inflated. The command of the Persian fleet had been jointly entrusted to Achaimenes, commanding the Egyptian vessels, and to Ariabignes who led the Ionian and Carian forces.

Many Greeks from the Persian-ruled Greek cities of the Ionian coast were also serving in the Persian fleet. On board the vessels were Persian commanders and military units of Persians, Sacans, and Medes. The purpose of these troops was to aid the sailors in their attacks against enemy ships and to prevent the crews from mutinying. The most serious problems faced by the Persians was the inexperience of their naval officers and the lack of confidence on the part

Scytho-Siberian style swords and daggers from the 5th and 6th centuries BC. (Scythian Treasures, National Archeological Museum of Athens, 1981)

of the crews, who had been forcibly conscripted and did not share the expansive ambitions of Xerxes.

Xerxes combined the counting of the army at Doriskos with an additional inspection of his forces. When the inspection was over, the Persian king called Demaratus, the former exiled king of Sparta, and asked him if he sincerely believed the Greeks would dare to fight against such a powerful army. Demaratus warned him that the Lacedaemonians, at least, would insist on fighting back and would never surrender. Xerxes found Demaratus' views on the determination and the fighting abilities of the Spartans unwarranted. So it was that the Persian army crossed

into Europe, with Xerxes absolutely convinced that he would defeat the Greeks with the sheer volume of his forces just as his ancestors had done, who had defeated and subjugated all the ethnic peoples that his campaigning invasion army now included.

The Persian king's army crossed the Evros River and then headed toward Pieria. Here it was delayed while routes were cut through the thick Macedonian forests. At Pieria, most of the messengers Xerxes had sent to the Greek cities requesting water and earth of submission met him. Xerxes now knew which cities had submitted to the threat of the Persian hordes and which ones were determined to resist him. The Greeks who declared their submission were the Thessalians, the Dolops and the Aenians, who lived in the south of Thessaly, and the Perraibians, the Locrians and the Malians, who lived in the Malian and the Euboean gulf areas. The Boeotians had also declared their subjugation, with the city of Thebes among the first to submit. An important exception among the Boeotians were the Thespians and the Plataeans who had refused to give earth and water from their soil to the Persian messengers.

The council in Corinth

While the Persians were marching on the European continent, the Greeks were preparing their plan of resistance. Representatives from all the Greek cities that had decided to resist gathered at Corinth in 481 BC to organize their opposition plans. The initiative to hold a Panhellenic council in Corinth had come from Sparta and enjoyed the support of the Athenians. All the Greek cities that had not yet submitted to the Persians were invited. Cyrene and Massalia were exempted from the invitation. The temple of Poseidon at Corinth was designated as the location for the council meeting. Ultimately, very few cities turned up to participate. The main participants were the representatives of the Spartans' allies in the Peloponnesus and from the two Boeotian cities trying to free themselves of Theban domination, Plataea and Thespiae. These two cities had allied themselves to Athens in order to resist their powerful neighbor, the city of Thebes. Additional city-states from mainland Greece participated in the council, but none of the distant Greek colonies in Italy, Sicily, and from the other

Mediterranean coastal areas showed any active interest.

At the initial discussion in Corinth, the Greeks did not manage to reach a final decision on the tactics they were to adopt. However, decisions were made during the council that constituted significant steps toward unity. The first resolution was to end all internecine wars, such as the mutual hostilities between Athens and Aegina, and to unite in the face of the common enemy. Representatives from many Greek cities made an oath of joint cooperation and decided on a chain of command, and thus the first great alliance among them was formed in order to ward off the foreign invasion. In the council's official decrees, its members appeared under the title "Hellenes" and enjoyed equal status. Each city had its own preliminary councilors (the probouloi) and the opinion of each city could be heard on an equal basis, regardless of the size of its populace, territory, or the military forces it could contribute to the common cause. Sparta was given the leading role in military matters, and it was decreed that the commanders of the alliance's army and naval forces would also be Spartans. The fact, however, that Sparta did not take advantage of the Persian invasion in order to impose its hegemony on the rest of the Greek states but agreed to accept equality among all the member cities of the alliance, reveals an advanced, shrewd policy in the face of the extreme dangers that threatened the freedom of the Greeks.

It was the first time that the Greeks had decided to put their local differences aside and create a military and political alliance with a common cause. The most important conflict that ceased to exist because of this agreement at the Council of Corinth was the war between the Aeginetes and the Athenians. In the past, these two cities had made profitable use of their differences as both had used the conflict as an excuse to reinforce their navies and to train their crews through important, firsthand experience in naval warfare.

The Greek cities also decided to send their envoys to Argos, the only Greek city that had not yet clarified its position on the issue of the Persian invasion. After Sparta, Argos was the next largest power in the Peloponnesus, so it was in a position to play a determining role in the final outcome of the struggle. Envoys were also sent to Sicily, to Gelon the tyrant of Gela, to Syracuse, to Kerkyra and to Crete.

The cities of the Greek peninsula had now sent a call for help to all the Greeks who might be able to aid them in the coming struggle. The Argives refused to contribute to the common cause, preferring to stay neutral, and used as a pretext the argument that they could not help if they were not appointed leaders of the alliance. The Spartans rejected their proposition immediately. Gelon was also not disposed to help the Greeks, as he was expecting an attack by the Carthaginians, the eternal enemies of the Greeks in the western Mediterranean. The Carthaginian cities were Phoenician colonies and their mother cities had informed them of the impending Persian invasion of Greece. They naturally thought the moment had arrived to attack the Greek colonies on Sicily, as the Greek mainland cities would not be in a position to come to their aid. A view has been expressed that the Carthaginians had made agreements with the Persians to undertake such an attack on the Sicilian Greek colonies. However, it is doubtful that Xerxes,

who was always arrogantly proud and assured of his own power, would ever ask for help from an ally who was free and not a subject of his empire. If Xerxes occupied Greece, Persia's aggressive expansionism would naturally turn to Sicily and Italy and this would, by necessity, cause a clash with the Carthaginians. The people of the island of Kerkyra promised to send help at first, but the promised help never arrived. Following the defeat of the Persians, the Kerkyreans claimed that they had prepared 60 triremes, but added that the weather had prevented them from reaching the Aegean. The Cretans also decided to remain neutral, citing the bad omens they had received from the Delphic oracle.

In the following year, 480 BC, when a new council was held at Corinth to decide on the tactics to be followed by the Greeks, representatives of the Thessalians, who were opposed to the agreements between the Aleuds and Xerxes, arrived in Corinth and requested assistance from the rest of the Greeks to block the narrow passage at Tempe and thus halt the descent of the Persians into lower mainland Greece. The cities present at the Council decided to send forces to Tempe. These forces arrived by boat at Alos, on the western coast of

A copper idol (eidolion) of a Spartan hoplite. The strangely shaped crest indicates officer status. (Archeological Museum of Sparta)

the Pagasetikos Gulf, and from there, crossed Thessaly on foot and arrived at Tempe. According to Herodotus, this army consisted of 10,000 combatants under the command of the Lacedaemonian Evainetos, while Themistocles, Athens' greatest statesman at that time, commanded the Athenian contingent. A large number of Thessalian cavalrymen also joined the force. It was hoped that they would be able to protect the passage from a barbarian attack, something that actual events later proved impossible.

King Alexander of Macedonia, who was obliged to follow the Persians on their expedition due to the location and weakness of his kingdom, tried to assist his fellow Greeks by providing them with secret information. He informed the Greeks at Tempe that the Persians knew of the existence of the second passage from Macedonia to Thessaly, at the present day site of Petra. The defenders of Tempe realized that to stay in the area any longer was pointless as they ran the risk of capture by becoming trapped in northern Thessaly, so they quickly retreated south. After the rest of the Greeks had departed, the Thessalians were no longer able to defend their land unaided and were forced to submit to Xerxes.

In the meantime, however, disputes had broken out among the Greek envoys still in Corinth. In general terms, the city representatives were trying to organize a common defense policy. The Peloponnesian cities argued that a wall had to be built across the isthmus to stop the Persians there. This argument did not, naturally, receive favor from the cities lying to the north of the isthmus, while many of the cities threatened to submit to Xerxes if the Peloponnesians did not help them to defend their soil. The Athenians believed that any defensive structure across the isthmus would be useless, since the Persians could, at any time, decide to invade any other part of the Peloponnesus by simply using their

The bronze head of a vulture from a pot of Asiatic origin. (Archeological Museum of Olympia)

fleet to outflank the isthmus. Their main concern was the control of the sea. A recent prophecy of the Oracle at Delphi had contributed to this Athenian view. The oracle had stated that the Persians, with the exception of "wooden walls," would occupy the whole of Attica. Many Athenians had interpreted this as meaning the ships of the Athenian fleet.

Finally, as the Persians approached, the weight of the defense rested on the shoulders of the few Greek cities that had decided to defend their freedom, despite their fear of Persian numerical supremacy, reprisals, and the revengeful punishment that awaited them in the event of defeat. The Spartans and the Athenians were the leading defenders. Most of the Peloponnesian city-state peoples had agreed to take part in the struggle, and these included the Corinthians, Tegeatans, Mantineians, Sicyonians, Epidaurians, Troizenians, Mycenaeans, Tirynthians, Phleiasians, Ermionians, and the Orchomenians of Arcadia. From the Hellenes living outside the Peloponnesus, the participants included the Aeginetes, Megarians, Plataeans, and the Thespians of Boeotia, the Phocians, Keans, Malians, Tenian, Naxians, Kythnians, Siphnians, Eretrians and the Chalcideans from Euboea. From the area of the Amvrakikos Gulf, where many Corinthian colonies existed, the defenders included the Leucadians, Anactorians, Amvrakians and the Aleieans, the Poseidaeats and the Lepreats. It is possible that, initially, more cities were coerced into joining the alliance due to fear of reprisal from the rest of the Greeks, but reversed their decision later when the impressive Persian army appeared. Since then, that first Greek alliance has remained strong in the memory of all the Hellenes. Later, when Phillip and Alexander were planning their Persian campaign, they considered themselves preservers of that alliance of the Council of Corinth. Those participants at the Council of Corinth never realized that it would become such a significant event in Greek history in the sense that it prepared them to oppose the Persians and was destined to help them to gradually change their long-held attitudes on relations among the various city-states and to unite in a common cause.

The Battle of Thermopylae
The titanic struggle of the Spartans and the Thespians against the Asian invaders

"The Final Stand": The few surviving Thespians and Spartans, many carrying broken spears, wounded and exhausted from the fierce battle, reached the crest of Kolonos Hill, carrying with them the lifeless body of Leonidas, where the Persians killed them all with arrows and spears. In the foreground is the body of Leonidas. At the lower left is his aide, wearing a wreath, which marks him as a winner of the Olympic games; his shield bears the emblem of the cult of Dokana. Behind the Spartan king is a Thespian warrior. (painting by Romilos Fronimidis)

The Battle of Thermopylae (480 BC) has a particular fame. Usually when historic events are described it is the victors who are praised. In the case of Thermopylae, however, the wreath of immortal glory belongs to the defeated, and it is the victors who usually stand accused for the cowardly manner by which they gained their victory against an army that was the embodiment of valor and devotion to duty.

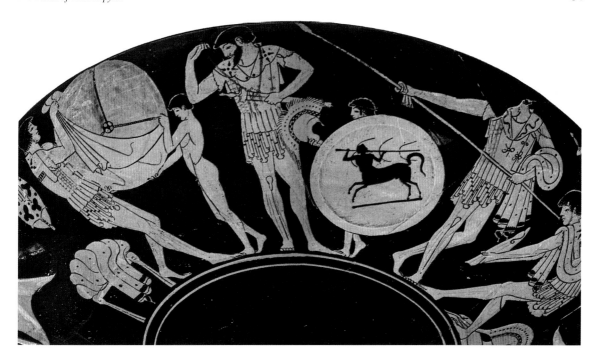

When the Persian army began its march south through Macedonia, the Greeks knew they could not expect help from the Greeks living on the coastal regions of the Mediterranean. Following the retreat from the Tempe passage, the decision was taken to position their forces at the narrow pass of Thermopylae, the "Hot Gates," which Xerxes' men had to traverse in order to reach Attica and the Peloponnesus. While the army stood at Thermopylae, the Greek fleet would gather at Artemisium in order to prevent the Persian fleet crossing the Euripus Strait. By so doing, the two Greek forces, army and navy, would be in close proximity and able to communicate easily. However, the two forces were interdependent, because if one of them retreated from its position allowing the Persians to move south then the second position would become untenable and would have to be abandoned to avoid being outflanked and encircled by the Persians. Furthermore, Artemisium and Thermopylae were the last

defensive positions before entering Boeotia and Attica and, if the Greeks proved unable to hold them, the Persians would march unopposed into Athens.

The Thermopylae pass

At the time of the battle, Thermopylae's ancient coastline was much closer to the foothills of the mountains than it is today. Only a very narrow passage existed that was easy to defend with a small army against a larger attacking force. According to various calculations, the additional silt and sediment deposits over the centuries have caused an expansion of the soil that has, from antiquity to today, moved the coastline a distance of 7 km further out. At the time of the Persian invasion, the narrow

Warriors preparing for battle. On the left, a warrior prepares his shield, assisted by a child. On the right, another warrior about to fix his greaves. The Spartans' meticulous grooming before the Battle of Thermopylae made a huge impression on the Persians. (5th century BC, The Vatican Museum)

The interior of a Greek hoplite's shield.

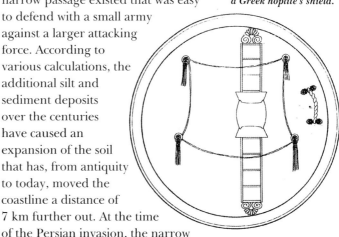

A sculptured relief portrayal of Xerxes.

passage between the mountains and the sea at Thermopylae was approximately 7 km long. Its narrowest points were at the entrance and exit and a horse-drawn carriage would find it difficult to pass through at these points. At the pass there was also an old wall that had been made by the Phocians to stop the raiding Thessalians. This wall had long been abandoned and lay in ruins, but the Greeks repaired it. The Greeks had decided to halt the barbarian invasion at this point. It was an ideal defensive location because the Persians would be unable to take advantage of their army's numbers or use their famed cavalry charges in such a narrow corridor. In addition, the surrounding mountains appeared impassable for an organized army.

The Persians approached the narrow passage from the western side, where the mouths of various rivers lay and where there was also a small plain on which the city of Trachis stood. To be more precise, the mouth of the Sperchios River lay in the most westerly part, and a small distance from there lay the mouth of the Dyras River, known today as the river of Gorgopotamos and a branch of the Sperchios River. At that time, the two rivers did not join but their mouths were very close to each other. Further to the east was the mouth of the Melas River, while a short small distance from that was the mouth of the Asopos River. The Asopos River plain defined the border between the small valley, formed by the mouths of the rivers, and the area of the Thermopylae corridor. The Persians set up their camp between the Melas and the Asopos rivers. The entrance of the narrow passage of Thermopylae lay a short distance from their encampment. From this point, the passage widened for a short distance until it reached another point, where it narrowed again. In the middle of these two narrow points there was another small town, Anthele. The Delphic Amphictyony used to hold its meetings there, and the two temples of Demetra and Amphictyon were part of this town. At the second narrow point was the wall built by the Phocians and, after that, the passage widened once again. It was at this point that the Greeks chose to set up their camp, as they wanted to be near the wall. After the Greek camp there was yet another last point where the way again narrowed considerably. To the east of this third point, and on the route leading to Thermopylae, near the village of Alpenoi, the Greeks set up their stores and provisions camp.

The Greek forces

The Persian army at Thermopylae had been reinforced by small contingents of Thracians, Macedonians, Thessalians and men from other neighboring races to the north of the narrow passage. All these had been obliged to submit to the Persians because the Greek alliance formed at the Corinth Council had not helped them to resist. For the Persians, the large volume of their army was more of a handicap than an asset in the narrow confines of the Thermopylae pass.

The opposing Greek force consisted of 300 Spartan hoplites, 500 Mantineians, 500 Tegeats, 120 men from Arcadian Orchomenos and an additional 1,000 Arcadians. There were also 900 perioikoi in the force of the Spartans. At Thermopylae, there were also 400 Corinthians, 200 Phleiasians, and 80 Mycenaeans. In addition, there were 700 Thespians and 400 Thebans from Boeotia. The Opuntian Locrians, who lived to the east of the passage, had sent all of their hoplites to Thermopylae.

In total, the Greek army gathered at Thermopylae did not exceed 7,000 hoplites. The contingent from each city had its own commander, but the overall commander was Leonidas of Sparta. At the time, a rumor had circulated that Thebes had made a secret pact with the Persians, and this was the reason why the rest of the Greeks had invited the Thebans to participate in the defense of the Thermopylae passage. The Thebans had, indeed, declared their submission to Xerxes and had revealed this fact to the other Greeks, but had sent only a small token force of 400 hoplites, under the command of Leontiades, to help. Indicative of the situation with the Thebans was the fact that the much smaller city of the Thespians managed to send a contingent of almost double that size. It was for these reasons that the rest of the Greeks mistrusted the Theban hoplites. The policy Thebes would follow with the Persians was not certain at all.

The forces assigned to the defense of the passage were small compared to what the Greek cities could, in reality,

provide. While the Locrians and the Thespians had sent a sizeable part of their armies, other cities had only sent very small contingents. For example, Corinth, although it had a large population, had sent just a few hundred hoplites. Sparta's case was similar, as it had sent Leonidas and his 300 Spartans and about 900 perioikoi. According to Herodotus, this situation can be explained because, at that moment, the Olympic Games were in progress and the cities preferred not to engage in war preparations under such circumstances. Furthermore, many cities believed that the clash at Thermopylae would augur the start of a long conflict with the Persians, and it was felt that a comparatively small force would suffice to repulse the initial enemy attacks until the rest of

A Greek hoplite's Corinthian helmet.

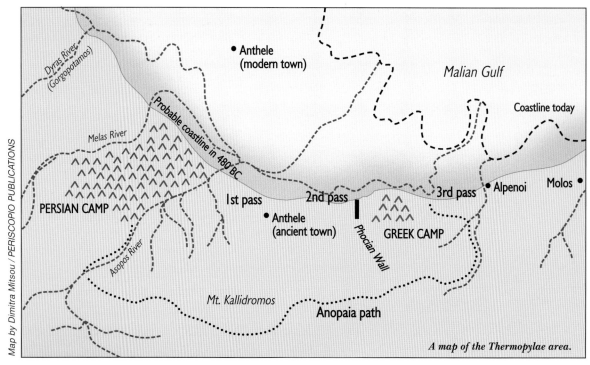

A map of the Thermopylae area.

A Greek hoplite departs for war. The illustration is based on one found on a red-figure amphora from the 6th century BC from the National Exposition of Antiquities of Berlin. (illustration by Romilos Fronimidis)

the Greek armies arrived. The Spartans, in particular, sent their small force in order to bolster their image. They feared they would be accused of cowardly indecision, so they decided to send Leonidas with just 300 hoplites to Thermopylae to convince the cities and communities of the area that they had the support of Sparta and thus gain their favor. They hoped to assure their position as the alliance's leader against the Persians and avoid the rise of a defeatist attitude among the Greek ranks.

When the Persians approached Thermopylae, it caused much agitation and excitement among the Greeks guarding the passage. The Peloponnesians were ready to desert and retreat to the isthmus. The reaction of the Locrians and Phocians was understandable, arguing that, in

A warrior from mainland Greece. The artwork captures the general image of the Locrian and Phocian soldiers who fought alongside the Spartans at Thermopylae. The warrior illustrated wears an archaic Corinthian helmet with impressive double crest holders (the red-figure pottery of the time also shows helmets with triple crest holders). His cuirass is made of flexible composite materials covered with metal scales on the outer surface. He wears bronze leg armor, and carries a large "hoplon-type" sword. The very archaic decorative designs on the shield show a continual spiral pattern (a symbol of fire), a right-handed swastika (a symbol of the unconquerable) and a four-spoke wheel (a symbol of the War God's chariot). (uniform research and reconstruction by Christos Giannopoulos)

that case, their lands would be left defenseless and they would be forced to surrender to Xerxes. Leonidas realized that a retreat would deal an irreparable blow to the alliance that had been formed at Corinth. The other Greeks were suspicious of the Peloponnesians and accused them of planning to desert in order to defend only their own lands at the isthmus. To dispel all such suspicions, the king of Sparta ordered his army to stand fast at Thermopylae and requested the neighboring cities to send more soldiers to reinforce the defenses of the Thermopylae pass.

A bronze statuette of a Spartan hoplite, made in Laconia in the 6th century.

While Leonidas was trying to bolster morale and maintain a cohesive force, Xerxes ordered a cavalryman to spy on the Greeks. The mounted Persian managed to reach the second pass near the Phocian wall, but as he was unable to pass that point and observe the Greek camp, he returned and reported only on the activities of the guards he had observed near the wall. At that moment, it was the turn of the Spartans to guard the wall. The spy was surprised to observe some of the men were doing physical exercises, while others were busy grooming their hair. Despite their small number, they did not give the impression that they were worried about the imminent battle. Also, when they discovered his presence, they let him continue watching them and allowed him to leave unmolested. No one had tried to pursue him. When Xerxes heard the spy's report he was impressed and called Demaratus, the exiled Spartan king, to ask him about these men, about the rumors circulating about them, and about their strange and inexplicable, at least to the Persian mind, behavior. Demaratus explained that it was the Spartans' custom to groom themselves and especially their hair when they were about to place their life in danger. He warned Xerxes once again that these men would prove to be the most able and most dangerous opponents he had faced until now. However, the Persian king continued to consider Demaratus' warnings exaggerated.

The first clashes

Xerxes was so convinced that his army would strike terror among the Greeks that he stayed in his camp for four days without ordering his men to attack. He still believed that when the Greeks realized how large the Persian force was, they would retreat of their own accord or surrender. In addition, it also gave him more time to gather additional information about his opponents, especially the Spartans. What he had heard about them had impressed him, though he still held the view that no army could stop a Persian force. After the four days had passed, however, Xerxes decided the enemies he faced were impudent and insane. He decided, therefore, to apply more pressure on his opponents, and sent messengers to Leonidas asking him to become his

Pottery of the Archaic period showing the Greek phalanx in battle. On the left can be seen a piper whose music gave the warriors a marching rhythm.

ally. In exchange, he promised to help him dominate the whole of Greece and the Greeks and make him an absolute monarch. In answer, Leonidas accused Xerxes of promising things that were not his own by right, stressing that he would rather die for Greece than become a monarch ruling over his compatriot Hellenes. Leonidas also emphasized that as a Greek, he had been taught by his ancestors to conquer lands through valor and not through cowardice. After receiving this answer, Xerxes again consulted Demaratus. The Persian monarch still felt confident that his army would succeed. He proudly boasted that the defenders of Thermopylae would have to run faster than his Persian cavalry in order to save themselves. Demaratus cautioned Xerxes to be more careful as what he had heard about the Greeks, and especially about the Spartans, did not at all appear unwarranted to him. Xerxes remained unconvinced and sent out one last group of envoys to

Leonidas. This time he demanded that King Leonidas surrender the Greek arms. Leonidas, making use of the characteristic laconic prose of the Spartans, urged Xerxes to come and take them. His famous answer "Come and get them" («μολών λαβέ») has become famous throughout history, and remains synonymous today with the undefeatable spirit of the defenders of Thermopylae.

Following Leonidas' second rejection, Xerxes ordered the Medes and Kissians to arrest his opponents and bring them to him in chains. The Persian king favored the Medes for this task because of their proverbial braveness on the battlefield, although it is also possible he may have wanted to dent their pride a little by assigning them a difficult mission. The Medes had dominated the Persians up to the time when Cyrus created the large Persian Empire. Despite the change of circumstances, the Medes retained their proud attitude and felt superior to their former subjects who were now

A Spartan hoplite strikes down his Persian opponent. An illustration based on a red-figure cylix cup from Attica of the Museum of Edinburgh. (illustration by Romilos Fronimidis)

their masters. Xerxes calculated that he would thus benefit whatever the outcome of the battle, as the Medes would either take the pass or they would be defeated and lose face. The order given to the Medes was to capture the impudent enemies blocking the path of the king of Persia and to bring them to him in fetters. Among their ranks, the Medes and Kissians included many relatives of men who had fallen at Marathon and sought revenge. Xerxes believed that the presence of such people among his forces would ensure that the troops would fight with a greater zeal.

When the Greeks saw the Persians preparing for battle, they took up position at the entrance of the first pass. Xerxes' warriors clashed against them in force but with no visible result. The barbarians kept attacking with successive charges, but were defeated each time by the Greek phalanx, failing to break through its impenetrable wall of shields and spears. In the narrow confines of the pass, the Persian ranks were tightly packed and each jab of the spear easily found a target. Of course, this tactical situation favored the Greek hoplites, who possessed better armor. Many Medes were slain without managing to break the Greek lines. The Greeks had formed successive lines of defense, according to their cities, and these lines alternated in the front line fighting, a tactic which gave the hoplites a chance to rest. The Persians were unable to gain any benefit from their numerical advantage and could not exhaust the Greeks with successive attacks by new, fresh troops. The pass resounded with the sounds of battle. The Greeks advanced in strict order, to the sound of the flute that gave the

THE FIRST DAY OF THE BATTLE OF THERMOPYLAE

Greek forces   Persian forces (Medes and Kissians)

The Medes and the Kissians cannot break through the Greek formation.

Map by Dimitra Mitsou / PERISCOPIO PUBLICATIONS

Malian Gulf

2ND PASS

Phocian wall

The Asopos river ravine at the point where the Persians, commanded by Hydarnes, began their march along the secret path. (History of the Greek Nation, Vol. 2)

A bronze statuette of a Spartan. (National Archeological Museum of Athens)

phalanx its marching rhythm and to the sound of the paean that was sung in unison by all the hoplites. The Medes and the rest of the Persian soldiery, on the other hand, marched under the lash of the whip and the insults of their officers. Each new Persian section that fell upon the first line of the Greek phalanx would turn and run off. The Medes would pause their charges every now and then, retreat to regain order and reform, and charge again, stepping on the dead bodies of their comrades that had piled up in front of the Greeks. None of their successive attempts bore fruit.

When Xerxes observed the Medes' repeated failures, he realized he was facing very dangerous opponents. As the Medes had failed in their first attacks on the Greeks, the Persian king now decided to use the cream of his forces for his next attack, his elite corps of "Immortals." This unit consisted of 10,000 elite Persian warriors who constituted the king's bodyguard. They were titled "Immortals" because if one among their ranks died or was forced to retire another elite soldier immediately replaced him. Hydarnes, son of Hydarnes, an eminent Persian, commanded the "Immortals." The uniforms and arms of the "Immortals" were highly decorated with gold and silver so they stood out among the others, and their corps enjoyed special additional privileges. On the fifth day of the confrontation at Thermopylae, and on the second day of the battle, the time had come for the "Immortals" to prove their fame and show themselves worthy of their privileges. Xerxes probably thought it a good opportunity to advertise the power of the Persians to the people under his rule. The superior race of

The Mt. Kallidromos peak dominates the Thermopylae landscape. (photo by D. Garoufalis)

A statuette of a Spartan hoplite. (National Archeological Museum of Athens)

the Persian conquerors would succeed where the Medes had failed, and thus prove its pre-eminence.

In order to face the Persian assault, Leonidas had placed the Spartans - the best of the Greek hoplites at Thermopylae - in the front ranks of the first line. His intention was to deceive the Persians by planning a feint that called for a move of a tactical retreat followed by a sudden counterattack. The use of such a tactic required perfect coordination on the part of the hoplites that only the Spartans could achieve due to their previous lengthy, hard training. The Spartans proceeded to pretend they were having difficulty repulsing the "Immortals" and, by feinting a retreat, begin to draw them farther in. As the battle neared the entrance to the first pass, the Lacedaemonians pretended they were unable to withstand the pressure and started to retreat toward the Phocian wall and the Greek camp. The "Immortals" were drawn in and advanced after them. However, the

Spartans maintained their order intact and led the Persians to a point where they would have a problem maneuvering with their large numbers of troops. When the "Immortals" entered the narrow space, the Spartans, with their formation still intact, suddenly turned around and attacked them with all their strength. Every tactical move by the Lacedaemonians was executed in perfect synchronized order, as if by a single entity. The Persians, unaccustomed to such a high level of training, were taken completely by surprise. Furthermore, their javelins were shorter than their opponents', and they were receiving wounds they could not answer. The Persians in the front ranks tried to retreat toward the pass exit but were blocked by the large numbers of their rear ranks. Meanwhile, the rear ranks, unaware of what was happening ahead, kept pushing the troops ahead urging them to advance. The shouts of the rear ranks were

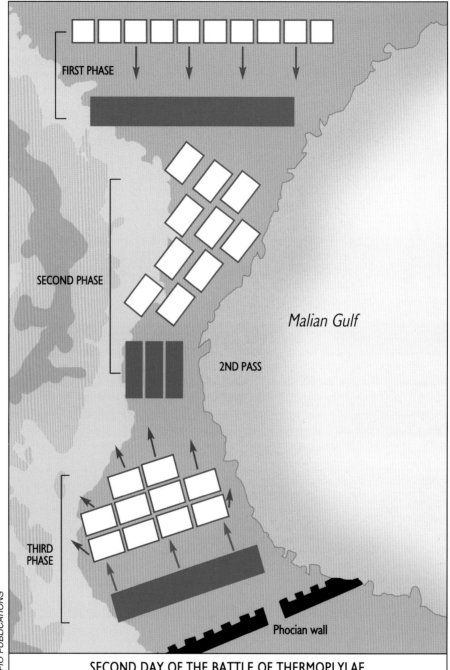

SECOND DAY OF THE BATTLE OF THERMOPLYLAE

Greek forces   *Persian forces ("Immortals")*

1st Phase: The "Immortals" attack the Spartans.

2nd Phase: The Spartans pretend they cannot take the pressure and retreat to the Phocian wall.

3rd Phase: The Spartans turn suddenly and attack in force, retaining their strict formation. The "Immortals" are surprised.

A Kissian shield bearer section leader (sparabara-paschadathapatis). The Kissians were considered descendants of the Elamites, a pre-Iranian race from the Persian Gulf, and, according to Herodotus, they were among the first to attack the Spartans at the Thermopylae pass. The section leader illustrated here is clad in typical Median fashion. His clothing includes a long-sleeved tunic and trousers featuring woven Eurasian patterns. His defensive armament consists of a large, spara-type composite shield and a padded linen cuirass that, according to Herodotus, resembled fish scales. His offensive weapons include a short spear and a short double-edged sword (akinakes), the latter suspended from his belt and tied to the right thigh. Herodotus writes that "the clothing of the Kissians was similar to the Persians," but on their heads, instead of soft caps, they wore turbans. (uniform research and reconstruction by Christos Giannopoulos)

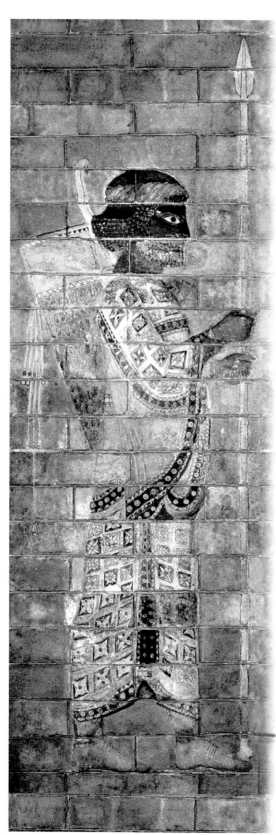

A Persian "Immortal" from the Palace of Susa.

mixed with the shouts and screams of the men of the front ranks who were fighting the finest infantry of Greece. When, finally, the whole "Immortal" phalanx realized it had to retreat, it was too late. They were unable to move in the confined space of the pass, and a great panic set in as soldiers trampled their colleagues as they pushed to get to the exit in order to escape. In the meantime, the Spartan phalanx was making headway into the Persian ranks like a wave of bronze and iron that destroyed everything in its deadly path. The famed "Immortals" had been trapped in the first pass of Thermopylae and had suffered great losses because of their inability to maneuver.

Xerxes observed the battle from a throne he had set up specifically for the purpose. During the battle, he jumped up three times at the sight of the heavy losses of his army. What was even more unbearable for him was the debacle suffered by his "Immortals," the cream of his Persian army, before the eyes of so many of his subjugated races.

On the following day, the Persians continued their attacks, but their morale was low. The previous day's failure had shaken their faith in victory, and they had discovered the weaknesses in their armament. Their armor was too light compared with that of the Greeks, and their spears were too short. Furthermore, in contrast to the Greek phalanx, they were not trained to fight in strict order and to maintain their formation lines intact. Despite realizing these shortcomings, they continued their attacks throughout the following day, acting under a combination of orders and the lash of the whips wielded by their commanders. They kept advancing toward the pass in waves, but their attacks had no effect on the defenders of Thermopylae. Like the previous day, the Greeks rotated the troops in the front lines and the barbarians had constantly to face fresh, well-rested opponents.

The only forces that did not take part in this rotational tactic of holding the pass were the Phocians. These had been entrusted with guarding a path that led from the Persian encampment on the plain to the rear of the two Thermopylae passes, near their exit, and close to the village of Alpeinoi, where lay the Greek provisioning camp. Initially, this path followed the Asopos River valley and then turned east near the foothills of Mt. Oete. From there, it led through Mt. Kallidromos on a parallel course to the northern coast. It continued at some distance from the coast and the Thermopylae pass and then met the valley of a small river and began to descend toward the village of Alpenoi. It was known as the Anopaia path. It is quite possible that the Greeks were not, initially, aware of the path's existence but only learned of it when they first arrived at Thermopylae and camped behind the old Phocian wall. If the Persians discovered this path, they could outflank the Greeks and attack their rear and thus trap them. The path, however, was narrow and, therefore, difficult to follow. Furthermore, an organized army could not use it without being seen. In addition, the Phocians, charged with guarding that area, would always be able to delay the enemy until the Greeks at the camp could be warned of the approaching enemy. The Phocians had positioned themselves strategically at the path's highest point to be able to survey the whole area around them.

The treason of Ephialtes

By the end of the battle's second day, Xerxes was enormously disappointed at the results. Seemingly, the Greeks had found a standing position where the numerical advantage of the Persians was proving useless, and their better training, armament and stricter discipline were to their extra advantage. The Persian ruler was at an impasse. To maintain his huge army in the area for a long period was not feasible, as they would soon run short of provisions. Conversely, he was not willing to order a retreat, as he did not desire to appear weak in the eyes of the subject races accompanying him. The solution

A helmet cheek guard showing a battle scene in relief.

A Spartan officer wearing his cloak. The artwork was based on a bronze statuette of the Wadsworth Artheneum Museum of Art. (illustration by Maria Ginala, based on research by Dimitris N. Garoufalis)

to his dilemma appeared suddenly. His bodyguards informed him that a resident of the area named Ephialtes had appeared at his camp and that he came from the city of Antikyra in Malis. He claimed he knew of a secret path in the mountains by which the Persians could get to the rear of the Greeks. Xerxes was enthused by the idea of gaining an easy victory and trapping his enemies who had dealt such a devastating blow to his army and to his prestige. He ordered Hydarnes' "Immortals," using Ephialtes as their guide, to follow the path that same evening. His plan was to have the "Immortals" in position at the rear of the Greeks by the following morning. At the same time, he planned to attack the entry of the pass from the other side with the rest of his army. Trapped in the pass between two enemy forces, the Greeks would suffer a terrible defeat that would serve as a dire warning to anyone daring to doubt Persian supremacy.

Herodotus writes that the "Immortals" set out from the Persian camp after sunset, just as the night torches were being lit. Throughout the night they made their way along the Anopaia path. Toward dawn, they approached the 1,000-strong Phocian hoplite force guarding the area. The Persians had hoped that the area would be guarded by a smaller contingent and that the Phocians would be unprepared. Indeed, the Greeks were unaware of the Persians' knowledge of the existence of the path, and it is possible the guard was not fully alert. The area was also thick with oak trees behind which the Persians must have found cover. The ground, however, was covered in fallen branches and leaves, and when the "Immortals" stepped on

A decarch of the Persian "Immortals" (amrtaka-pascadathapatis).
This is one of the most heavily armed warriors from the first line of the
elite corps of the "Immortals." The term 'amrtaka' is believed to be the
ancient Iranian name for the "Immortals," while in ancient Persian
texts can be found the term "pascadathapatis," signifying the leader of
a ten-man section. His defensive armor consists of a full-height
"spara" type shield (what Herodotus called "geras"), made of a
series of wicker reeds covered with leather sections, and he wears
a flexible scale, cuirass-type armor covering the whole of his
torso. His offensive weapons are the spear, bow and
arrows for open field battle, and the short, gold-
handled sword known as akinakes. The warrior's
gold torque-like necklace reveals that he is a
free native Persian warrior and not
a subject from a conquered country.
(uniform research
and reconstruction
by Christos Giannopoulos)

them they caused a crackling noise that was immediately detected by the Phocian guards. There was no wind that morning. The guards sounded the alarm, and in a short while all the Phocians had taken up their arms and stood ready to face the enemy.

Hydarnes was surprised at seeing the path guarded by such a large force, and was worried he might have to face the fearful Lacedaemonians. Ephialtes reassured him by telling him that the force guarding the path consisted of Phocians. The Persians then decided to engage and ordered their archers to launch a cloud of arrows against the Greeks. In answer, the Phocians immediately retreated to higher ground to protect themselves from the rainfall of Persian arrows. They thought the Persians would follow them and were determined to die there and retreat no further. But, as they had retreated to higher ground, they left the Anopaia path uncovered. That was the opportunity the Persians had awaited, for instead of continuing the battle at this point, they began to run along the path toward Thermopylae. Time passed and a new day started to dawn. The Persians had left the Phocians on the elevated ridge knowing that, from there, they would be unable to prevent their rapid descent to Thermopylae and to the rear of the Greeks.

A bronze statuette of a Greek hoplite from Dodone, possibly the work of an Athenian craftsman. (Archeological Museum of Ioannina)

The Greek reactions

In the Greek camp, the men had just risen and the soothsayer, Megistias, was performing the usual morning sacrificial rites. Herodotus states that the internal parts of the slaughtered animals warned that on that day the defenders of the pass would face death. After a short while, news reached the camp that the Persians had discovered the Asopaia path, that they had bypassed the Phocian guards and were nearing their position. This news caused agitation and was soon transformed into dangerous rumors. Leonidas immediately called a meeting of the commanders of all the forces from the various cities. Some were already leaving the passes as soon as possible in order to save their forces. Others, however, held the view that the battle had not yet been lost and they could stay and resist. A retreat from the passes would mean eventually surrendering to the Persians the whole region from Thermopylae to the isthmus. Also, it was possible the Persian forces coming through the Asopaia path were small in number, as the path was unsuitable for a large army. Still, some men felt unsafe, and a number of troops from some cities were already leaving. The remaining forces announced that they were determined to remain at the pass and continue the battle under Leonidas' command.

The king of Sparta judged that not everybody had to remain at the passes. If, ultimately, the Persians managed to surround them, their losses would be far too great, and Greece would lose many of its defenders. Now that the enemy was crossing Mt. Kallidromo and the defense of the pass seemed useless, the cardinal priority was to save the army. To this end, Leonidas

A depiction of the Persian Royal Council. (National Museum of Naples)

ordered the remainder of the Greeks to depart. He and his Spartans would remain and fight at Thermopylae to the death. According to Herodotus' appreciation, Leonidas was afraid of the defeatist spirit that overcame some Greeks when they discovered the enemy was approaching from an unexpected point and was threatening to encircle them. And since he now no longer had any confidence in their will to continue the fight, he preferred to let them go. Herodotus also states that the Spartans had received an oracle from Delphi stating that the only hope to avoid Sparta being occupied and destroyed by the Persians was the death of one of its kings. Leonidas thus decided to sacrifice himself in order to save his home city, doing as the oracle had decreed. Herodotus also writes that the rest of the Greek forces departed as soon as they heard of the Spartan king's decision, with the notable exception of the Thespians who declared their wish to remain at Thermopylae and share Leonidas' fate. The Thespians' commander was Demophilus, the son of Diadromos.

The Thebans also elected to remain, although it appears that this may have been against their will as, claimed Herodotus, Leonidas did not allow them to leave as he considered them hostages rather than allies. As the general impression was that at the slightest opportunity the Thebans would desert and join the enemy, their presence as hostages in the Greek camp guaranteed that their city would continue to be part of the Greek alliance against the Persians.

Herodotus' writings concerning this matter seem contradictory and confused. On the one hand, he presents Leonidas as sending away the rest of his army because he deemed them to have adopted a defeatist attitude, while on the other hand he retained the Thebans at Thermopylae when these were considered the most undependable section of the Greek army because of the contacts they had formerly made with the Persians. Plutarch later accused Herodotus of unfairness and falsehood in his writings about the Thebans. In his essay on the malice of Herodotus,

An illustration of a fully armed "Immortal." He is armed with a spear with a butt in the shape of an apple, a short sword of the akinakes type, a bow and arrows and a lushly decorated large shield known as "spara". He wears a rich scaled cuirass over his colorful garments. Instead of a helmet, he wears a classic Persian tiara, which was not very protective. (uniform research and reconstruction by Christos Giannopoulos)

A black-clad Thespian. The warrior illustrated here is representative of the 700 Thespians who fought to the last man at Thermopylae. During the 5th century BC, the emblem of the city of the Thespians was the half moon of Black Aphrodite on a Boetian shield. The worship of life-giving force, represented by Aphrodite and Eros, was a central theme in Thespian religious belief. Each piece of this Thespian warrior's armor is in the color of mourning and darkness and shows his belief that he will march into a battle never to return. (uniform research and reconstruction by Christos Giannopoulos)

Plutarch criticizes the historian for all manner of prejudices and misrepresentation. According to Plutarch, keeping the Thebans as hostages would have proved dangerous for the Spartans and Thespians as the Spartan hoplites would have the double task of keeping an eye on the Thebans and facing the Persians. Plutarch's conclusion was that the assumption that "Leonidas did not retain the Thebans because he did not trust them" cannot be true. For Plutarch, the information given by Herodotus, who had spent a major part of his life in Athens writing his works, had been distorted over the years by Athenian narratives. Herodotus had gathered his information on the Medic Wars from various narratives on the part of Athenians who hated the Thebans and had most likely presented a totally distorted image of the reality. Plutarch finally concludes that the Thebans stayed because Leonidas thought they were battle-worthy. While Plutarch's argument seems plausible to a certain degree, it does not negate the fact that the ultimate actions of the Thebans justified the suspicions held against them.

The texts of Herodotus contain some more contradictions. If Leonidas deemed the passes indefensible, why did he not retreat? Herodotus states that such a retreat would be have been a blow to Sparta's image. It is true that Spartan law did not permit its

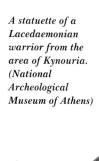

A statuette of a Lacedaemonian warrior from the area of Kynouria. (National Archeological Museum of Athens)

citizens to desert in a battle and leave their fellow warriors uncovered. Prior to a battle, however, the Spartans were allowed to leave one particularly dangerous position in order to avoid certain defeat. The spirit of Spartan law was to assure a high performance in battle and retain an efficient, organized Spartan army, but not to lead that army to total destruction. The Spartans very rarely deserted a position. When they did so, it was only after a very careful examination of the tactical situation from which they concluded that there was no other option left.

A different view of these events exists that aids us to better interpret the issues Herodotus' description has created. According to this view, Leonidas did not lose heart when he was informed of the approach of the Persians but prepared a plan to trap them instead. This plan provided that the Spartans were to remain with the Thespians at the Thermopylae pass and wait for the appearance of Hydarnes' "Immortals." The rest of the Hellenes were to retreat a small distance and wait. When the Persians arrived at the entrance to the pass, they would face the Spartans and the Thespians and think they had encircled the whole of the Greek forces. Then, with the "Immortals" engaged with the Greeks in the pass, the rest of the Greek army would attack them from the rear. In the end, this final part of the plan did not materialize, perhaps due to defeatism among the rest of the Greek forces, who lacked the courage to return to the pass and assist those who had been left behind.

According to the above theory, the Spartans reserved for themselves the most dangerous and honorable task, as was their custom. They wished to have the Thespian hoplites beside

The monument to the 700 Thespians who fell at Thermopylae. (photo by D. Garoufalis)

them because there were quite a lot of them and they had clearly distinguished themselves in earlier battles. In all probability, the Spartans considered the Thespians their most trustworthy ally with whom to share the most dangerous part of the plan, the defense of the pass. Furthermore, they felt close to the Thespians as, according to mythology, they shared a common ancestor as both peoples were considered descendants of Hercules. The Spartans, however, retained the Thebans because they did not trust them. Leonidas had heard the various rumors on the wavering attitudes of Thebes and was justifiably suspicious that if he allowed the Thebans to leave for their city, they would cause problems to the rest of the Greeks and deal a blow to the morale of the army. Also, it was possible that the Thebans might warn Xerxes of the trap Leonidas had set for him. If, on the contrary, the Thebans remained at Thermopylae, they would be a lesser risk and they would be under the surveillance of both Leonidas and the Thespians. The Thespians were the Thebans' neighbors and had differences, and

their mutual interests clashed. In addition, certain smaller Boeotian towns, like Thespiae, were attempting to gain their autonomy from Thebes, a city that sought to dominate all of its adjacent regions. Another most likely possibility is that the Persians had promised the Thebans the domination of Boeotia in exchange for their cooperation. The above theory, despite the fact that it does not derive from the official sources, seems quite credible.

The start of the final clash

Xerxes waited until late morning before ordering his army to attack. Ephialtes had proposed this time as he estimated that Hydarnes' force would then be nearing the rear of the defending Greeks. The Greek hoplites saw the Persians approaching and advanced to the widest section of the pass, to a position they had not yet fought in («Επί θανάτω έξοδον»). During the previous days, they had preferred to fight at a narrower point to allow them better control of the area.

The fact that they had decided to fight at a wider part of the pass proves to Herodotus that they were certain of their imminent death. Until that time, the Greeks had chosen to fight near the wall, but this was now useless as the Persians had outflanked their position by using the mountain path. The barbarian hordes were now able to cross the first pass and begin their advance toward the Greeks. Behind the Persian soldiers came officers with whips urging their men forward by whipping them and shouting threats and insults. As the Persians advanced into a narrow section, some on the outer side fell into the sea while others were trampled by their fellow troops as the mass tried to squeeze into the narrow path. The Persian army, however, continued its inexorable advance toward the standing Greeks.

The Greek hoplites on the far side had formed a defensive line and had their spears and shields at the ready. The barbarian flood filled the pass and was fast approaching. When the first

waves arrived before the Greek line, they hesitated and slowed down. Those at the very front tried to protect themselves from the Greek spears but those following them pushed them forward. As there was no room to turn, many barbarians were killed instantly because they had no time to react, their shorter spears could not reach the Greeks, and their lighter armor provided no protection. Despite the continuous enemy pressure, the Greek phalanx remained steadfast. As their spears broke from overuse, the Greeks drew their swords and continued the battle. However, by this time, the barbarians had been pushed closer to the Greek ranks, and because the blows they now received were more effective, this led to even greater losses. Although the Greek ranks were now at a disadvantage, undaunted, they continued to fight back. The Spartans had been trained since they were youth to withstand the pain of war. The Thespians also showed a tenacity and strength that possibly

The battlefield area of Thermopylae today. All the area to the right of the motorway was covered by the sea in 480 BC leaving only a narrow passage. (History of the Greek Nation, Vol. 2)

A Spartan hoplite. There was a certain uniformity in Spartan battle dress during the Persian Wars. All hoplites wore red clothing and a bronze, bell-shaped cuirass. Linen armored cuirasses had not yet become universally popular. They also wore greaves, carried a hoplon shield and wore a closed Corinthian helmet. Particular differences could be spotted on shield emblems (which were related to certain units or "morai") by the shape of the crest holder or the decorative patterns woven on the soldier's tunics. (uniform research and reconstruction by Christos Giannopoulos)

came from the hard agricultural work they were used to on their native Boeotian plain. Amongst the many dead barbarians were some of Xerxes' relatives, including his brothers Abrokomes and Yperanthes. In addition, many more had lost their lives at the hands of the Greek phalanx because they had tried to satisfy the vanity of their king in order to gain his favor.

Greek losses were equally serious. Leonidas had fallen in this first phase of the battle. A hard struggle between Persians and Greeks had taken place around his dead body. The Persians tried to carry away the Spartan king's body, as they knew that Xerxes would richly reward whoever brought it back. The Spartans, on the other hand, considered it a matter of honor to protect the body of their king and not let it be desecrated by their enemies. The Spartans protecting Leonidas' corpse managed to repulse the enemy four times, but as the struggle was reaching its peak, Hydarnes' "Immortals" arrived.

The final phase of the battle

The appearance of Hydarnes' forces changed the Greek tactics. The Spartans and the Thespians

A bust of a Spartan hoplite thought to be that of, and known by the name, "Leonidas."

retreated to the narrowest point of the pass, hoping to retreat farther to their camp before the "Immortals" had a chance to join with the other Persian forces. After passing the Phocian wall, the Greek forces came to the top of the Kolonos hill, next to the Greek camp. Their intention was to continue to fight from there until the last man had fallen.

Years later, the Greeks erected a marble lion sculpture at that point in honor of Leonidas. The retreat proceeded in an orderly fashion with the phalanx retaining its formation. Herodotus adds that the Thebans did not follow the rest of the Greek but chose instead to surrender by advancing toward the Persian lines with outspread arms, shouting that their city had been among the first to offer water and earth to Xerxes' envoys. They claimed they had been brought to Thermopylae against their will by the threats from the other Greek cities. The Thessalians serving in the Persian army were quick to confirm the Theban's claim, saying it was true and so most of them avoided a certain death sentence. However, the Persians mistakenly killed a number of Thebans as they tried to surrender due to the confusion that reigned. The rest were led to the Persian camp where, following Xerxes' orders, they were branded with the symbols of royal power including Leontiades, their leader. Branding had a special symbolic significance, as it was used primarily as a punishment for slaves who had escaped. As the Thebans had declared their submission to Xerxes and then subsequently joined the Hellenes in the war against him, they received the same treatment.

The Persians remaining in the narrow pass followed the retreat of the Greek phalanx, with the "Immortals"

The ruins of "Leonidas' tomb" in Sparta.

joining them a short while later. In the meantime, the defenders of the pass had reached the top of Kolonos hill, exhausted from the battle, carrying broken spears, and a large number of wounded warriors. They had decided to continue fighting with swords, but the Persians were afraid to go near and preferred to attack them with their bows and arrows from a safe distance. Xerxes' losses were already too heavy, and he would not allow more men to be the sacrificed for the destruction of a few desperate warriors still fighting against all odds and certain defeat.

The Spartans were weak and exhausted from their desperate efforts, and were bleeding from their many wounds. Their swords and spears were broken in pieces, but the savage, tiger-like ferocity that energized them continued unabated until the last. They fought with tooth and nail when all other weapons failed them, and finally crumpled to the dust at last in convulsive and unyielding despair. Their struggle did not cease until all were slain, with every limb of every man ceasing to move. Their leader Leonidas had already fallen.

The last surviving Greeks had been killed by a rain of arrows and spears.

When all the Spartans and Thespians had fallen, Xerxes ordered his men to find Leonidas' corpse, decapitate it and place the head on a wooden pole. This caused revulsion among many Persians who had a high respect for bravery. Xerxes' act confirmed for some their view that the Great King's deeds were always exaggerated and his acts would more than likely bring the wrath of the gods against him.

Xerxes' next worry was what course his military operations would now follow. His army was now free to invade Boeotia and Attica. Athens, the hated city that had supported the Ionian Revolt and had humiliated the Persian army at Marathon, now stood unprotected.

Xerxes once again asked Demaratus' opinion of the course to take to continue his conquest of the country. Demaratus replied that he did not think the king could easily gain possession of the Peloponnesus by marching to it directly, because the opposition he would encounter at the isthmus would be formidable. There

FIRST PHASE

Malian Gulf

2ND PASS

Phocian wall

SECOND PHASE

THIRD DAY OF THE BATTLE OF THERMOPYLAE

 Greek forces
(Spartans, Thespians, and Thebans)

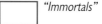 "Immortals"

 Persians

1st Phase: The Greek hoplites advance into the wider section of the pass and attack the Persians.

2nd Phase: The Thebans surrender. The Spartans and the Thespians retreat to the Kolonos hill where they are eventually surrounded by the "Immortals" and other Persian forces and slain under a rain of arrows and spears.

The monument to the 300 Spartans at Thermopylae. (photo by D. Garoufalis)

The statuette of a warrior, possibly Spartan, from the area of Dodone. (Archeological Museum of Ioannina)

was, however, he said, an island called Cythera, opposite the Spartan territories, and near the coast, which he thought the king could easily take. This might then become the base for future operations for the reduction of the whole peninsula, as bodies of troops could be dispatched from it to the mainland in any numbers at any time. He advised Xerxes to send 300 ships to Cythera, a move calculated to frighten the Laconians, as with such a strong threat close by the Spartans would not dare leave their homeland and assist the other Greeks. There was also the possibility that the perioikoi, (the free but noncitizen inhabitants of Sparta) and the helots would rise against the Spartans and would thus make it easy for the Persians to dominate the rest of the cities. However, Xerxes' cousin, Admiral Achaimenes, stepped in and declared that the Persian fleet would thus be separated in two and the Greeks would be able to confront it more easily. It would leave the fleet, he told the king, a miserable remnant, inferior to the enemy, for they had already lost 400 ships in storms. After hearing these conflicting opinions, Xerxes decided to follow his admiral's advice and not to launch a naval assault against Laconia in order to keep his forces united. This decision was destined to have unpleasant consequences later.

Conclusions

From the time of the battle to this day, there have been many interpretations regarding the causes that led the Thespians and the Spartans to their sacrifice. At various times throughout history, certain regimes have used the battle to justify sacrifices on the part of their military.

The first such instance was by the very same Spartans. After the Persians had departed Greece and Xerxes' threat had found its nemeses at Salamis and on the plain of Plataea, Sparta and Athens found themselves competing for the hegemony of Greece. The Laconian city praised Leonidas' and his 300 warriors' sacrifice to the highest degree in order to justify its demand to become the leader of Greece. Many military bodies and academies have acted likewise, promoting the example of the sacrifice of the Thermopylae defenders as the

The statue of Leonidas at Sparta.

highest proof of devotion to duty and honor. Even today, the hoplites that fell at Thermopylae are seen as ideal soldiers and as eternal examples of bravery for military men of all epochs to imitate. At various times throughout world history, many views have been expressed on the matter of the sacrifice of the defenders of the pass. Some of them have been original, others offensive, some fictional, and others extremist.

To interpret the behavior and the views of the Hellenes, it is essential that we understand how they related to their city-state. Every Greek belonged to a city-state. Exile from one's city and exclusion from its community was unbearable to many of its citizens. The city was important as it guaranteed its citizens the most valued gift - their freedom - and in an environment in which the values of moderation and civilization dominated. Freedom, by itself, was not such a valuable concept. The barbarians living in Scythia and in the northern areas of the Balkan Peninsula were also free. However, they lived in an inferior way, because their kind of freedom was a limited one where the strongest enjoyed privileges at the expense of weakest, and no law existed to restrict this freedom. In Asia, on the other hand, despite the wondrous civilizations there, a law existed that governed the behavior of the citizens. This law was the power and will of a dynasty that repressed huge populations. It was for this reason that the peoples of Asia were considered inferior by the Greeks, despite the rich civilizations they had developed. The uncivilized nomads of the Scythian steppes were seen in a similar light. Freedom in the world of the Hellenes was based on a fine balance between freedom itself and the restrictions of law that existed in a city-state. In a city-state, the citizens could have a direct relationship with those exercising power and could control them directly or indirectly. This was possible because of the small size of the city-state, which was a manageable unit and did not spread over huge areas as did the Persian Empire. It was this kind of freedom that the Spartans and the Thespians defended at Thermopylae against the annihilation Xerxes had threatened.

Much has been written in the past regarding the behavior of the **defenders** of Thermopylae and, probably, much more will be written in the future. The truth may never be uncovered, and the interpretation of the battle **and of** the sacrifice of the Thespians **and** the Spartans might continue to puzzle researchers seeking explanations for centuries to come. Without doubt, the Thermopylae defenders were not driven by a self-destructive zeal, neither did they have the slightest desire to abandon this world because they considered it vain. What is certain is that ancient Greek civilization was founded on the principles of love of life and for the beauty of this world, as can be seen in the way that the Greeks depict men and nature in their art. The classical aesthetic was based on the love of this world and dominated the arts. Still, there were a few things that were considered more valuable than life. Chief among them was the preservation of freedom and moderation in everything. Xerxes had threatened both of these values with his arrogant, proud behavior. When these two values were in danger, then sacrifice was a necessity, even if it were seen as the lesser evil. For the Greeks, life and death were part of a wider system of values on which their behavior and their fame depended. In Ancient Greek religion, people after death were equal. All ended up in the darkness of Hades where they wandered as former shadows of themselves. However, there always existed the possibility that a dead man might enjoy better fortune if he remained alive in the memories of men, and this very concept constituted the highest form of life after death for the ancient Greek - to be cited by the following generations as a symbol and an heroic example to imitate in the same manner as the Homeric epic heroes were often cited. In order to reach that level of fame, one had to live and die in a particular way and the defenders of Thermopylae had already achieved that.

Artemisium
The Greek navy's first battle against the Persian fleet

While the hoplites under Leonidas' command heroically defended the Thermopylae pass, the Greek triremes scored their first naval victory over the Persian fleet at Artemisium. Although these naval operations were overshadowed by the Battle of Thermopylae and the heroic sacrifice of the Spartans and Thespians, they were of great significance. At Artemisium, the Greek fleet managed to successfully protect the flanks of the defenders of Thermopylae and, thereby, set the tone for the final victory at the naval battle of Salamis.

Simultaneously, along with the heroic defense of Thermopylae, another battle for the defense of Greece was taking place in the sea passage between northern Euboea and Magnesia. During the Persian army's advance into Greece, the Persian fleet at all times sailed as near to the land forces as possible. Xerxes had adopted this tactic, as he wanted to keep his forces concentrated and under strict control. The Persian headquarters staff was also afraid of disaster from storms at sea. If such a disaster did occur, the army's morale would suffer, the provisioning supply chain would be broken, and communication with Asia would be cut. The fleet was also

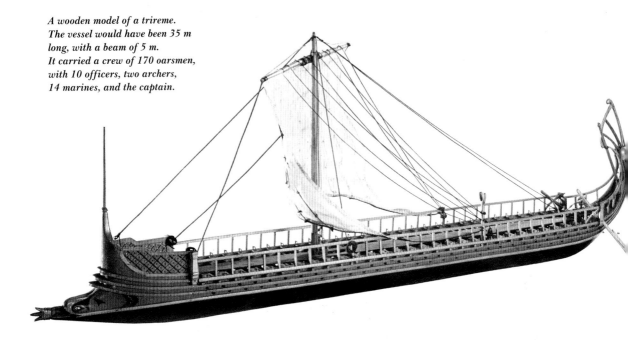

A wooden model of a trireme. The vessel would have been 35 m long, with a beam of 5 m. It carried a crew of 170 oarsmen, with 10 officers, two archers, 14 marines, and the captain.

Athenian marine. The only surviving color depiction of an Athenian marine comes from a wall fresco at the Elmeli funerary monument in Asia Minor. This 5th century fresco in combination with contemporary red figure pottery provided the evidence for this illustration. The majority of the Athenian hoplites and marines appear to have worn composite cuirass armor made of white linen and leather decorated with red piping. The Athenian marine at Elmeli is shown wearing a Corinthian helmet with a red and white crest and a blue tunic. The single-edged broadsword and the shield emblem are based on red figure pottery showing the Athenians fighting the Persians. (uniform research and reconstruction by Christos Giannopoulos)

*A vase painting
of a trireme about
to ram a larger vessel.*

valuable as it provided the king and his court with a quick means of escape from Greece in the case of a total defeat or mutiny in his armed forces. Mutiny was improbable, but the Persians could not be certain what would happen among the subjugated peoples if the invasion failed. A similar attitude of Persian suspicion prevailed for the Greek ships within the Persian fleet. Most of their crews were from Phoenician cities or from Greek areas in Asia Minor. All these Hellenes mistrusted the Persians, had revolted against Persian reign two decades earlier and, under the present circumstances, were obliged to fight their fellow Greeks. These considerations had led Xerxes to the decision to maintain his fleet close to his army where he could keep an eye on both.

Regarding the number of Persian vessels, many hypotheses have been advanced. According to Aeschylus' tragedy "The Persians" and to Herodotus' texts, the Persians had 1,207 ships, 207 of which were equal to the Greek triremes in speed and maneuverability.

The Persian army and fleet began their advance together from the Thermaic Gulf. They then went separate ways, the army entering inland Thessaly and the navy sailing along the Magnesian coast. It had been arranged that the Malian Gulf would be their next meeting point. The advance of the Persian army into Thessaly met with no particular obstacles or resistance as the Greeks had, by then, given up their plan to make a stand at Tempe. The fleet, however, had to sail around the northeastern side of the coast to the west of Mt. Pelion. It was there that northerly winds created problems for the ships, as their Asian captains had no previous experience with the currents and the wind forces that could be encountered in the Aegean. This particular coast had no safe anchorages for such a sizeable fleet. In the end, and after four days of rough sailing, the Persians managed to arrive in the Pagasetic Gulf and to anchor in the safe harbor of Aphetai.

During the voyage, and for the first time in its history, the Persian fleet encountered Greek ships. These were reconnaissance vessels, sent to the northern Aegean area by the Hellenes. However, off the island of Skiathos, three Greek ships sailed within reach of ten Persian vessels and were captured. This mishap was a bitter blow for the morale of the Greek crews.

The Greeks at Artemisium

Cape Artemisium, where the Greek fleet had gathered, lay opposite the anchorage of the Persian fleet. It had been named after the temple of Artemis that was situated in the area.

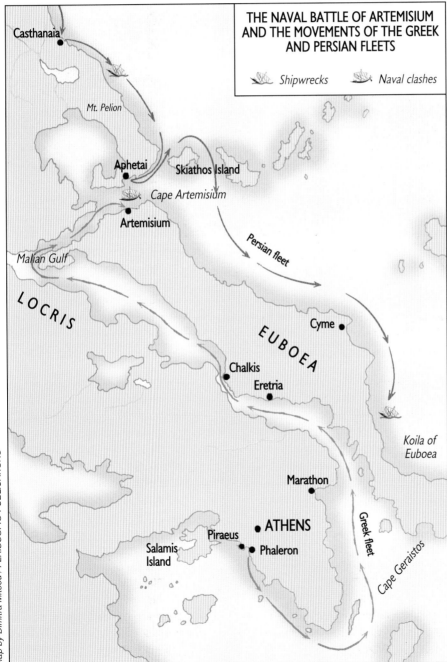

THE NAVAL BATTLE OF ARTEMISIUM AND THE MOVEMENTS OF THE GREEK AND PERSIAN FLEETS

⚓ *Shipwrecks*   ⚓ *Naval clashes*

Casthanaia

Mt. Pelion

Aphetai

Skiathos Island

Cape Artemisium

Artemisium

Malian Gulf

Persian fleet

L O C R I S

E U B O E A

Cyme

Chalkis

Eretria

Koila of Euboea

Marathon

Greek fleet

ATHENS

Piraeus

Salamis Island

Phaleron

Cape Geraistos

The trireme "Olympias" of the Greek Navy is a seaworthy, faithful replica of an actual ancient Greek ship.

Herodotus states that the Greek fleet was composed of 271 triremes and nine pentaconters. The Athenians' contribution to the fleet amounted to 127 triremes, with 20 additional triremes crewed by Chalcideans. Further south, in the Euripus strait, the Athenians had 53 additional triremes held as a reserve force. The purpose of this reserve was to guard the strait separating Euboea from Boeotia, thus avoiding a surprise of the enemy sailing round the Aegean side of Euboea and heading north to Artemisium. Eurybiades, from Sparta, was the admiral commanding the Greek fleet. Some had argued that Sparta should have given the naval command to its second king as Leonidas was the commander of the Greek army at Thermopylae. However, the Spartans believed that the best course was to retain one of the two kings in Laconia to run the

internal affairs of the state and keep an eye on the behavior of the helots and the free but noncitizen inhabitants of Sparta. The Spartans preferred to fight on land and only accepted the command of the fleet for reasons of formality, as they were also commanders of the Greek alliance. Unfortunately, Eurybiades was not as open-minded as Leonidas, and was unable to gain the trust of the Greeks with his attitude and behavior with the same ease as Leonidas had done. The Spartan admiral had a narrow, nationalistic attitude that evoked an adverse reaction among members of the alliance, especially among those who came from cities outside the Peloponnesus. Because of this, Themistocles, who was at that time the leading statesman in Athens, commanded the Athenian fleet and had been responsible for the organization and development of the

Athenian navy, overshadowed Eurybiades' role. Indeed, when, following the Battle of Marathon, silver was discovered in the soil of Laurion, it was Themistocles who persuaded his fellow citizens to use the profits from the mined silver to build a fleet, instead of following the original plan of sharing it among themselves as a form of bonus on the part of the state. Because of this, when the new Persian threat appeared, the Athenian fleet was ready to face it.

Before the Battle of Artemisium, Themistocles had managed to create a series of naval outposts along the coasts of Euboea, despite Eurybiades' disapproval. Through them, he maintained communications between the army at Thermopylae and the fleet, while also gathering intelligence information. The mastermind behind this network was Amvronichus, the son of Lysicles, one of Themistocles' admirers and friends. The gathered information was immediately sent to Themistocles, who was thus better informed than the Spartan admiral. The information was then processed and circulated among the crews of the vessels in a revised form so there was no risk of damaging their morale. Control of information was necessary because, as long as the Greek fleet was close to Thermopylae, Themistocles had to maintain a balance among the conflicting attitudes of the many commanders from the various cities. Some of them, especially the ones from the Peloponnesus, wanted limited tactical maneuvres with very few offensive actions, aimed only at protecting the naval forces flanks. Others desired daring, offensive actions against the Persian fleet. In consequence, Themistocles had to

compromise between the two extremes, and attempt to strike a balance in order to apply his own tactical solution. His objective was to protect the land forces at Thermopylae and prevent the Persian ships from entering the Malian Gulf. He also intended to cause the greatest possible damage to the Persian vessels through offensive actions whenever the opportunity presented itself.

In order to stop all the dangerous,

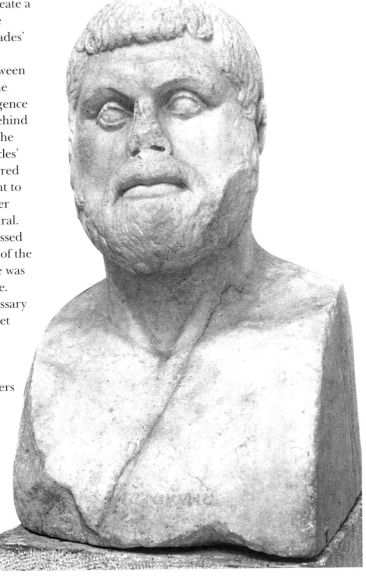

A Roman copy of a bust of Themistocles. (Ostia Museum)

extremist plans of offense, Themistocles leaked out some information calculated to cause apprehension. However, a number of Peloponnesians in the fleet used this information as an excuse to seek a retreat to the isthmus. When this proposal became known, the Euboeans reacted unfavorably because if the fleet retreated now, it would become unprotected from Persian attack. To this end, they offered Themistocles 30 talants to make him keep his ships at Artemisium. The Athenian admiral now had to use all his diplomatic skills in the handling of these people. With the Euboean money, he bought the support of the trireme captains from the various cities. At the same time, Themistocles applied all the pressure and used all possible means, from persuasive argument to direct blackmail, on the rest of the naval commanders. In his efforts, he was greatly aided by the strict screening of military information that Amvronichus had applied. It was finally decided to keep the fleet at Artemisium for as long as the land battle at Thermopylae lasted.

The initial naval operations

Themistocles was aided by the weather and luck. A squadron of 15 Persian ships was forced away from the rest of the fleet by high seas, so these were easily captured by the Greeks - a morale - boosting success. The captured crews, the first Persian prisoners from all the operations up to then, were sent to the isthmus. This propaganda success had to be shown to as many Greeks as possible in order to motivate them to resist, and to make them believe in the ultimate victory. In the meantime, the commanders of the Persian fleet decided to blockade their

adversaries at Artemisium. A force of 200 Persian warships was ordered to sail around Euboea. On arrival at the Euripus strait, the captains of these vessels were to relay the order that the Persian fleet in the north was to commence its attack on the Greek fleet. If all went according to plan, the Greek ships would then be forced to retire toward Chalcis, where the southern section of the Persian fleet would be lying in wait. The Greeks had, however, been informed of the Persian plan through the information network that had been set up by Themistocles and Amvronichus. Themistocles then ordered the Greeks to launch an initial attack on the Persian ships in the afternoon in order to gain a first impression of their opponents' abilities and tactics. When the Persians saw the Greeks attacking, they felt certain of an easy victory because of the small number of Greek warships.

The Persian fleet started to close the distance, meeting the Greek ships halfway between the anchorages of the opposing fleets. The Persian warships succeeded in encircling the Greek ships, but the latter quickly reformed, made a circle with their rams pointing outward at the Persian ring and made successive attacks to try and break out and circle to the rear of the Persian warships. The clashes continued until sunset, when both sides disengaged. This naval battle was a great victory for the Hellenes, with approximately 30 Persian vessels captured.

Toward sunset, the weather turned stormy. The Persian fleet retreated for the night, and all 200 Persian ships still sailing around Euboea were destroyed in a sudden, violent storm that same night, floundering and sinking in the dangerous, coastal area known as Koila. The storm also spread additional destruction among the

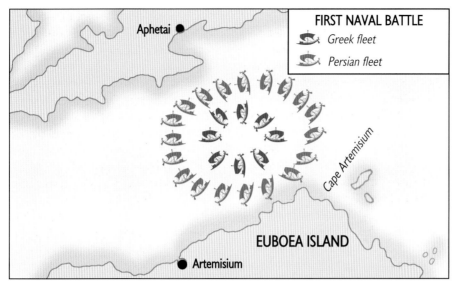

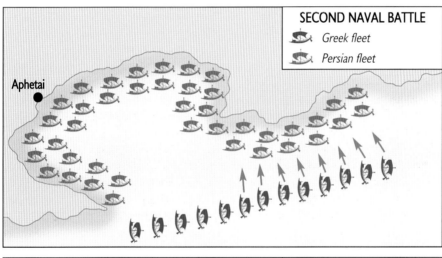

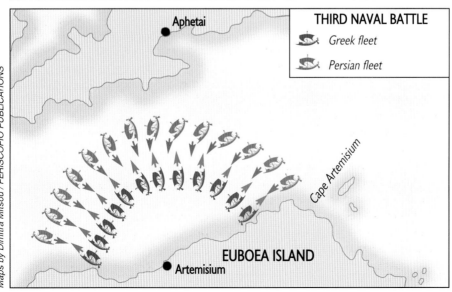

*A model of a trireme.
(Maritime Museum
of Greece)*

ships lying at anchor at Aphetai, as it blew the previous day's shipwrecks into them. The next day, the 53 Greek Athenian ships lying in reserve at Euripus, sailed to Artemisium bringing with them the news of the destruction of the Persian squadron to the rest of the fleet.

Following this failure, the Persians decided against any further operations until they had repaired the damage to the ships that had suffered in the storm of the previous night. The initiative had now passed to the Greeks. In the afternoon of the same day, the Greek fleet launched a new attack on those Persians that had

remained anchored at Aphetai. The Greek vessels managed to approach and destroy the Cilician ships lying on the outer side of the bay. Following this success, the Greek fleet sailed at full speed to Artemisium, with the Persians not making the slightest effort to pursue them because night was approaching.

On the following day, the Persians attempted to regain the initiative. At noon, their whole fleet weighed anchor and sailed from Aphetai. The Greeks, meanwhile, chose to remain at Artemisium so they could use the narrow waters to their advantage. Eventually, the two opposing fleets found themselves facing each other in two semicircular formations. The Persians tried to entice the Greeks toward the middle of the straits with the intention of encircling them again, or to force them toward the shore and trap them there. The Greeks had placed the outer ships of their formation very near to the coasts at each side, a tactical move designed to prevent encirclement by the Persians. The ensuing battle was particularly ferocious, with both sides suffering grievous losses, and no clear winner emerging. Half the Athenian vessels were damaged, while the Egyptian warships of the Persian fleet captured five other Greek ships. Included among the Greeks who distinguished themselves during the engagement was Kleinias, Alcibiades' father. The more maneuverable Greek ships caused great losses among the Persian fleet, although the latter, due to their greater numbers, managed to retain their formation and avoid defeat. All things considered, the Hellenes appeared to have gained the upper hand in this naval engagement, as, once again, they had achieved their goal of preventing the Persian fleet from sailing to the Malian Gulf. As the sea battle ended, a triconter arrived with Amvronichus on board who announced the fall of the Thermopylae pass and the heroic death of its defenders. There was no reason now for the ships to remain at

Cape Artemisium, as the defense of Thermopylae was no longer possible.

Themistocles revealed his strategic supremacy once again. He withdrew by using a series of tactical moves calculated to create confusion among his adversaries. He ordered his ships to approach all the points where the Persian warships were likely to anchor for victualing, and left clear messages to the Ionians and the other Greeks serving in the Persian fleet. In these messages, he asked them not to fight their fellow Hellenes and urged them to cause problems for the Persians at every opportunity that presented itself. Regardless of the effectiveness of these messages on the Greek crews of the Persian ships, the Persians' distrust of their Greek sailors reached a new peak.

So it was that the Greeks departed Artemisium as the actual victors. They had succeeded in blocking the Persian fleet's sea passage for as long as the land forces still fought at Thermopylae. Furthermore, they had caused great damage and losses among the Persian units. After Artemisium, the morale of the Greek crews was quite high, as they now knew they could defeat the Persians because of their better tactics, allied to the better speed and the maneuverability of their triremes. The Greek crews were determined not to let a victory slip away the next time they met their enemies.

The historical picture of the Battle of Thermopylae

The eternal example of heroism

The battle of Thermopylae has never been considered "just another battle," but has, since antiquity, always enjoyed a special significance. It was a defeat, but a glorious one, as it was the result of the voluntary sacrifice of 300 Lacedaemonian and 700 Thespian warriors. Military defeat was thus turned into an unprecedented moral victory, becoming the symbol of self-sacrifice for one's country and the defense of sacred ideals and values. In short, serving a high cause became synonymous with the battle of Thermopylae during the ensuing centuries.

Lacedaemonian hoplites of the later Archaic period (6th century BC). The warriors depicted wear Corinthian helmets, greaves, and bell-shaped cuirasses, and they carry swords and shields. The shields are decorated with the emblems of a scorpion and a cock, which represented certain Spartan army units. The helmets with one- or two-color reversed crests are believed to denote kings or officers. (uniform research and reconstruction by Christos Giannopoulos)

The Greeks living at the time of the Battle of Thermopylae attached great importance to the sacrifice of their compatriots. On the tombstones of the dead they carved the epigrams of the lyric poet Simonides of Ceos (556-468 BC). The first epigram refers to the Peloponnesians who fell in the first two days, prior to the departure of the rest of the Greek army. The numerical disparity of the forces of the opponents is emphasized, thus stressing the bravery of the Greeks. The epigram reads:

"Here once fought four thousand Peloponnesians against three million Persians."

In Greek:

«Μυριάσιν ποτέ τῇδε τριηκοσίαις εμάχοντο εκ Πελοποννήσου χιλιάδες τέτορες».

A second epigram was carved by Simonides himself on the tombstone of his friend Megistias, the soothsayer from Acarnania, who had volunteered to stay and fight alongside Leonidas' warriors:

"This is the tomb of the famous Megistias, slain by the Medes when they crossed the Sperchios, the soothsayer Megistias who knew well death approached but refused to abandon the king of Sparta."

(Herodotus, VII, 228).

In Greek:

«Μνῆμα τόδε Κλεινοίο Μεγιστία, ον ποτέ Μῆδοι Σπερχειόν ποταμόν κτείναν αμειψάμενοι, μάντιος, ος τότε Κήρας επερχομένας σάφα είδως ουκ έτλη Σπάρτης ηγεμόνα προλιπείν».

Another epigram of Simonides revealing the spirit of the Greeks was carved on the tomb of Leonidas' 300 warriors and constitutes one of the most famous examples of lyric epigrams in the history of literature:

"Oh stranger, Go tell the Lacedaemonians that we lie buried here, obedient to their orders."

In Greek:

«Ω ξειν, αγγέλλειν Λακεδαιμονίοις, ότι τῇδε κείμεθα τοίς κείνων ρήμασι πειθόμενοι».

(Herodotus, VII, 228).

One more epigram of Simonides about the battle reads:

"Those fallen at Thermopylae had glorious fortune and a good death.

Their tomb stands altar-like, in eternal memory instead of mourning grief.

Their fate stands as praise. A tomb inscription as this neither devouring time nor rust can erase. In this tomb of brave men lies Greece's brightest glory. Leonidas, the king of Sparta, having left us the great wreath of glory and the immortal fame of virtue, testifies."

(Diodorus, XI, 11, 2).

In Greek:

«Των εν Θερμοπύλαις θανόντων/ ευκλεής μεν α τύχα, καλός δ' ο πότμος,/βωμός δ' ο τάφος, προ γόων δε μνάστις/ο δ' οίκτος έπαινος./Εντάφιον δε τοιούτον ουτ' ευρώς/ούθ' ο πανδαμάτωρ αμαυρώσει χρόνος./ Ανδρών δ' αγαθών όδε σηκός οικέταν ενδοξίαν/ Ελλάδος είλετο, μαρτυρεί δε και Λεωνίδας/ ο Σπάρτας βασιλεύς, αρετάς μέγαν λελοιπώς/κόσμον αέναόν τε κλέος».

In another text, Simonides gives us the following appreciation of the dead warriors:

"The black cloud of death found them, but though slain, they will not die because the glory of their virtue will always bring them to the upper world from the houses of Hades."

(FGE 99b: The Palatine Anthology Z 251).

Leonidas the First (540-480 BC), the king who fought and died at

Thermopylae, was the son of Anaxandridas. In the first decade of the 5th century BC, he married Gorgo who bore him a son named Pleistarchos.

Leonidas thus found himself in the same situation as the 300 warriors of Thermopylae, as all of them had left a son behind at Sparta to preserve their family lineage. The name Leonidas, derived from the noun "Leon" (Lion), was common in Sparta, as in that city bravery and excellence in war were the highest virtues.

The site of the heroic sacrifice of Leonidas and his men became a reference point for the ancient Greek world. Shortly after the battle, a marble lion monument was erected at Thermopylae as an artistic dedication to the memory of the fallen king. Leonidas' body, or its remains if we accept Herodotus' assertion that it was cut in pieces by the Persians, was brought to Sparta around 440 BC and buried there with honors. In cases of funerary ceremonies for deceased Lacedaemonian kings, it was the usual practice to clean the body and cover it with a coat of honey or wax before wrapping it in a shroud. Xenophon writes that, in Leonidas' case, a model of his body was prepared for burial while special ceremonies proper for dead kings were held. Herodotus further comments that these ceremonies were exaggerated by common Greek standards, and he likens them to the burial customs of the Scythian barbarians.

These ceremonies included the announcement of the burial ceremony throughout Spartan territory, so that the greatest number of Lacedaemonians would attend, from all classes, including the helots and the perioikoi. This was a state ceremony, and the motivation behind it was to

"After Thermopylae": Ancient and contemporary Greek warriors shown with a British Commonwealth soldier. ("Punch" magazine)

emphasize the existence and strength of the Spartan city-state. The city itself halted all public activities for the period of the ceremony, and a ten-day mourning period was declared. There were even some cases where debts owed to the city were annulled and slaves were freed. All such moves were indicative of a common spirit toward internal unity among members of the same free citizen class and showed an attitude of generosity toward the ruled classes.

With the ceremony, the city of Sparta showed its political will to attach a special significance to the person of Leonidas. The timing of the movement and burial of Leonidas'

The portrait of a Spartan officer. (illustration by Christos Giannopoulos)

remains is also of interest. In 445 BC, a few years prior to the burial, a 30-year Peace Agreement had been reached between Athens and Sparta. In Sparta, there existed two opposing political factions, those desiring peace and those desiring war. The burial of Leonidas, a leader who had fought a national enemy, was possibly an attempt to reconcile both factions with the ultimate aim of achieving a climate of political unity and social stability. By this act, Sparta confirmed its military importance at a time when its role was close to taking second place to the Athenians' powerful Anti-Persian activities. Gradually, the Spartans' view of the primary mission of their city was changed to a new attitude in which the defense of the common freedom of all Hellenes was replaced by the preservation of the political autonomy

of Greek cities against the expansive intentions of the Athenian democracy (1).

The example of Thermopylae was so significant that Athenian orators used it to incite people to heroic actions. Lysias the orator reminded everyone of the heroic stand of the Spartans in the Persian Wars in his work "Olympian 7" with the intention of criticizing its protyrant foreign policy. In the late 4th century BC, Lycourgos, who was Anti-Macedonian in spirit, cites Thermopylae as an example of heroic action ("Against Leocrates" 106-7, 128-30). He even opined that the Athenians ought to exhibit the same attitude and to oppose Macedonian expansion in southern Greece. During the same period, Ephorus, from the Ionian city of Cyme, describes the sacrifice of the

Leonidas. A hypothetical representation of the heroic king based on the famous statue in the Sparta Museum. This is considered to be a portrayal of Leonidas (a view questioned in recent years). There are no distinctive uniform features setting him apart from a mere hoplite - a normal situation in a society where all men were lifetime warriors of the front line. The king's Corinthian helmet is based on that found on the statue, and features unusual cheek guards in the form of a ram's head. Horned animals did not only symbolize bravery in battle, but also indicated an aristocratic warrior's descent from a god. Leonidas was considered a descendant of the demigod Hercules and, therefore, of Zeus, father of the gods. His shield is decorated with the head of Gorgo, the female demon, whose terrifying glance turned her enemies into stone. The impressive figure of Gorgo often appears on Spartan shields and symbolized the aggressive spirit and qualities of leadership of Spartan women. Leonidas' dynamic wife was named Gorgo, a name which would be considered offensive in other Greek city-states. (uniform research and reconstruction by Christos Giannopoulos)

Lacedaemonian warriors at Thermopylae with high praise in his historical writings (FGH iia, no. 70). We also have many well-known epigrams from the Hellenistic period that praise the dead of Thermopylae and are ascribed to Hegemon and to Phainus. ("The Palatine Anthology," section 7)

The deceased kings of Sparta continued to be treated by free citizens of Lacedaemon as heroes, in essence as demigods. In Hellenistic times, the Spartans erected a permanent monument in their city and named it Leonideion. They also established the "Leonidaea," an annual festival of celebrations in honor of Leonidas. The festival only lasted until the late Hellenistic period, due to the decline of Sparta as a major power.

This celebration was reinstated, however, by the Roman emperor Traianus (98-117 AD), who re-established it as a kind of cultural ceremony. Honoring the ancient opponents of the Persians, Traianus reintroduced it during the 2nd century AD, during the period when the climate of enmity toward the Parthians, also an enemy from the east, who were, for the Romans, identical to the Persians. To be more precise, the celebrations were made possible because of the financial support of a cultured Roman benefactor under the characteristic name of C. Julius Agesilaus. The way in which the Romans gave titles to their nobles reveals the reverence the Romans felt toward Lacedaemon, the state by the Eurotas River and its military achievements.

The citizens of Sparta retained their remembrance of Spartan participation in the Pan-Hellenic efforts against their common enemies during the Persian Wars. In addition to the Leonideion monument, there were other monuments. One was dedicated to the 300 of Thermopylae, one to Pausanias, one was the tomb of Admiral Eurybiades, and another was a Persian stoa in the city's market. All these monuments belonged to the same wider group celebrating Laconian military valor.

During Roman times, Diodorus of Sicily (90-21 BC) praised the heroic actions of the defenders of Thermopylae with these words: "Who, from the later generations, would not envy the bravery of such men, who found themselves in the turbulent fight against a superior power, but stayed undefeated in soul and spirit even though their bodies perished" (XI 11,2). The Roman writer Seneca (4 BC-65 AD), one of the Stoic philosophers, proposes disdain of death as a way to live and cites as his example the 300 warriors of Thermopylae (Epistulae Morales lxxxii, 20).

Pausanias the Geographer also writes relevant comments in the middle of the 2nd century AD. In his work "Laconics" (IV, 7-10), he states: "The Greeks, of course, waged many wars among themselves, just as the barbarians had done, but few were made famous by the glory of one man like the glory of Achilles at Ilium and Miltiades at Marathon. It seems to me, however, that the achievement of Leonidas far exceeded in value all earlier or later heroic actions. Xerxes, the proudest king of the Medes and the Persians, could easily have been stopped by Leonidas and his few men as he marched against them. Xerxes would not have been able to seize the city of Athens nor burn it if that Trachinian (Ephialtes) had not led the forces of Hydarnes along the path of Mount Oetoe, and thus allowed the barbarians to encircle the Greeks and enter Greece after Leonidas' death."

Pausanias, as a writer, adopts the ideas of the Second Sophist School, which was a cultural movement that sought the restoration of the glorious political past of ancient Greece within the framework of the Roman Empire. Plutarch (46-120 AD) a member of the Second Sophist School, wrote a biography of Leonidas that, unfortunately, has not survived. In his work "Laconic Mottoes," Plutarch contains various dicta of Leonidas and sees his moral attributes as models for imitation. We find the same admiration for Leonidas in Plutarch's "Lives" and in the writings of Cleomenes the Third (326-221 BC).

The ironic Laconian writer Lucian (120-180 AD) adopts the opposite view. In his work "Teaching Oratory," he devalues the heroic ideals of Thermopylae and he also describes the degradation of moral values observed during the late 2nd century AD in certain sections of the Greco-Roman world. This degradation was more obvious in the eastern regions of the Roman Empire as, in Laconia itself, the preservation of the memory of the heroic stand at Thermopylae was a natural process and was included in the administrational processes of the city of Sparta.

The apologian writer Origenes (circa 185-253 AD) had a completely opposite view that was dictated by the new Christian teachings. According to Origenes, in moral and historic terms, the sacrifice and death of Jesus Christ can be likened to the voluntary sacrifice of Leonidas for the benefit of the larger community ("Against Celsus," ii, 17.404). The founding principles of the heroic ideals of Medieval Christianity originate in this view. No further references to Leonidas exist in the ensuing Byzantine period.

European opinion from the Renaissance to the 20th century

From the Renaissance onward, many foreign travelers visited Greece. In the 15th century, Ciriaco d'Ancona, an Italian merchant traveler, visited the city of Mystras. His visit was in 1447, when Constantinople had not yet fallen to the Ottoman Turks. In Mystras, the Italian visitor "recalls the glory of ancient Sparta and of its king Leonidas and wonders where those heroes have gone" (2). One can easily imagine what instigated this thought. The Despotate of Mystras, in common with the other remnants of the Byzantine Empire, was under siege by Asian Turks and this constituted the same eternal and familiar threat from Anatolia. This time, the target was the whole of Christianity and the threat had to be beaten off with the kind of bravery the Lacedaemonians had shown in the past. Sparta, in effect, had become synonymous with Greek patriotism against the Turkish menace. The Italian writer Petrarch (1304-1374) had already reminded his readers of the Thermopylae battle by writing of the "deadly pass defended by Leonidas with his few men" (Rime, xxviii, 100-1).

The memory of Thermopylae was also kept alive by the continuous and extensive study of the ancient Greek texts that characterized the Renaissance as a movement. Epigrams about Leonidas exist in the works of Luigi Alamanni, a friend of Machiavelli. During the 16th century, the Scot historian and humanitarian, George Buchanan (1506-1582), in his work "De jure regni apud Scotos" (1579), praises King Leonidas and other ancient kings of Sparta as real and gifted leaders who met the high demands of their time and culture. During the same period, the French writer, Michel de Montaigne (1533-1592), in his strangely titled study "De Cannibals" (1580), writes, "There are triumphant defeats that can compete with victories. Salamis, Plataea, Mycale and the Battle of Himera in Sicily are the most famous victories of which we know, but the glory of all these victories added together could not equal the glory of King Leonidas' and his men's defeat at the Thermopylae pass."

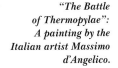

"The Battle of Thermopylae": A painting by the Italian artist Massimo d'Angelico.

Leonidas also reappears as a major historic figure in a work titled "Dialogues des Morts" by the liberal French writer François de Salignac

Fenelon (1651-1751). Fenelon praises Leonidas as a historic personality who sacrificed his life for the good of the community, an event that was rare in contemporary life. Leonidas is presented as saying to Xerxes, "I was a king whose sole task was the defense of my homeland and the unhindered enforcement of its laws." As the 18th century was a time when many conflicting political theories existed on what an efficient governing system should be, the personality of Leonidas loomed as the prototype of moral and political excellence because of his beliefs that had always favored the common people and because of his sacrifice at Thermopylae.

In England, the first reference to

A statuette of a Spartan warrior. (Archeological Museum of Ioannina)

Thermopylae in recent times was in Thomas Southern's play "Pausanias," staged in 1696. The music for the play had been composed by Henry Purcell (1659-1695). In this play, the heroic stand of Leonidas is set against the doubtful attitude of General Pausanias. Another, better known work, is Richard Glover's epic poem in praise of liberty named "Leonidas" published in 1737. In the poem, Leonidas is portrayed as a great patriot who chooses self-sacrifice for the good of his people, in contrast to the Persian leader, Xerxes, who is portrayed as the embodiment of insult, degenerate wealth and imperial power. In his work, the Persian Empire symbolizes the ambitious political forces in France at the time, as these forces sought to establish an overseas empire at the cost of England, a power struggle that was later to lead to the Seven Years War (1756-1763).

The depiction of the battle of Thermopylae in the visual arts was influenced by the classicism that dominated the late 18th century. Classicism was closely connected to the French Revolution, and its subject matter focused on the themes found in classical antiquity (3). The heroic attitude became one central theme of European thought, and within that general philosophy the battle of Thermopylae held a key position.

When the conflict brought about by the French revolutionary forces opposition to other European politics began in 1792, the French identified themselves with the Thermopylae defenders. One general of the French Revolutionary Wars, Charles François Dumouriez, who guarded the passes of Valmy, stated that he was fighting at a new Thermopylae and expressed the hope that his fight would have a better end. In the autumn of 1793, the town of St. Marcellin in the region of Isère was temporarily renamed Thermopyles, and in 1794 a play was staged named "Combat des Thermopyles," in which Leonidas is not portrayed as a king but as a brave general, in accordance with the political ideals of the time. In the French play, the Spartans defeat the Persian Empire. This historic misinterpretation is related to the French successes against Imperial enemy forces.

The French Neoclassical painter Jacques-Louis David (1748 - 1825) considered to be the foremost painter of the time, painted his famous picture "Leonidas at Thermopylae" in 1814, an exquisite composition depicting the Lacedaemonians just before the final clash. The depiction of Leonidas is a refined one and reminds one of the glory of past wars. David was Napoleon's favorite painter. The French Empire (1801-1815), ruled by the Corsican-born emperor, often commissioned works of art with references to the glorious past, mainly from the years of the Roman Empire. Of interest is the correlation of the subject of this painting with the critical situation of France at the time. One of Napoleon's aids, Bertrand Barère de Vieuzac, in his work, "Mémoires de Bertrand Barère" (1843 iv, 174), commented on the painting, "All the Spartans were slain in the Russian campaign. Their defeat amounts to a new Thermopylae." After Waterloo (1815), Barère attempted to reconcile the monarchists with the Bonapartists. Addressing the French soldiers, he spoke of the Battle of Thermopylae as a struggle for both the defense of the king and of the laws of the state.

The Greek Revolution of 1821 revived the Philhellenic Movement throughout Europe. Frequent references to Sparta were made in the form of historic analogies as the Turks were portrayed as the new Persians, and the people of the Mani as the new Lacedaemonians. This analogy is seen in numerous works of the period (4). The most famous example is the tragedy "Leonidas" (1825) written by Michel Pichat. The principal hero of the play is Leonidas, who announces prophetically that the memory of ancient Sparta and of its gallantry in wars will be revived.

The triumphant reception the tragedy enjoyed, according to its writer, was the fact that the French "saw Markos Botsaris as a new Leonidas and his heroic death reminded them of the heroism shown at Thermopylae." A final reference from the 19th century exists in the poetry of Victor Hugo in his poem "Les Trois Cents" (1873), where the despotism of the Persians is set against the spirit of freedom and self-sacrifice of the Spartan warriors.

The works of the English poet Lord Byron (1788-1824) also include references to Thermopylae. In his narrative poem "Childe Harold's Pilgrimage" (1812) he writes:

"Sons of the Greeks, arise!
Sparta, Sparta, why in slumbers
Lethargic dost thou lie?
Awake, and join thy numbers
With Athens, old ally! Leonidas recalling,
That chief of ancient song,
Who saved ye once from falling,
The terrible! The strong!"
In his other long poem titled 'Don Juan', Byron calls for a new Thermopylae against the Asiatic Turks:
"Earth! Render back from out thy breast
A remnant of our Spartan dead!
Of the three hundred grant but three
To make a new Thermopylae."

"The death of Leonidas at Thermopylae."
A model vignette in 54mm scale showing an allegorical depiction of the death of Leonidas. The model kit (Product No: SGS06) is manufactured by the Spanish model company Andrea Miniatures. A wide selection of armor, clothing and weapons are represented, including linen and muscle cuirasses, greaves, circular shields, spears, swords, and Corinthian helmets with cheek guards. Some aspects of the model have been converted, and the modeler's artistic license, although gaining a better effect, has strayed from strict historical accuracy. The kit itself is complete with all four Greek warriors and a fallen Persian and consists of 44 metal parts and a resin base. (The photo is courtesy of Andrea Miniatures)

(Don Juan. Canto iii. Stanza 86. 7.)

Elsewhere, Byron, like the French writer Pichat, likens the heroic death of Markos Botsaris with Leonidas' sacrifice at Thermopylae, proof that the Greek spirit had not faded with the passage of centuries.

Another poet of the same period, William Haygarth, claims that the tradition of Thermopylae is still alive since:

"even the spirit of the Spartans
walks on the earth
the clang of their arms
echoes in the hills of Mani."
(Greece, A Poem, 1814)

The Greeks, during the Revolution of 1821, reminded many of the ancient Lacedaemonians. In general, the British intelligentsia of the 19th and 20th centuries showed a marked preference for Athens, a naval power and a democratic state, rather than for Sparta, a land power and an oligarchic state. One exception was the British Tory party during the latter half of the 19th century, which promoted the study of Sparta in middle and higher education schools and universities. The battle of Thermopylae, however, continued to be influential in the 20th century. Archeological finds by the British School of Archeology

contributed greatly, as a marble statue thought to represent Leonidas, was unearthed in Sparta. It is more probable that it represents a god from the pediment of a building, although it is still commonly described as a statue of Leonidas.

The image of Leonidas' 300 was also used at the beginning of the 20th century by members of the Irish Republican Army (IRA). In one of its revolutionary songs, "A Nation Again," it is stated that the Irish fought like Leonidas' 300. In this case, the British

Empire replaces the Persian one, and the Irish, who were fighting for national independence and freedom from British rule, become the Thermopylae Greeks.

In the German world of Letters and the Arts, the historical portrayal of Thermopylae and the Spartans underwent many changes. In the transition to the 19th century, the values of the French Revolution were influential, and Sparta was seen as the embodiment of oligarchic political systems. "Hyperion" (1797-9) was one

The statue of Leonidas at Thermopylae. (photo by D. Garoufalis)

of the early poems of Friedrich Hölderlin (1770-1843), a fervent admirer of ancient Greek culture. In this poem, Sparta's military nature is closely connected to Greece's struggle for independence. This effort fails, however, and the memory of the bad turn of events after the Orloff Revolt of 1770, when the Greeks rose against the Turks and failed, haunts the poet (5).

The philosopher Johann Gottfried von Herder (1744-1803), in his work "Ideen zur Philosophie der Geschichte der Menschheit" (Ideas for the Philosophy of History of Humanity), written in 1784-91, considers the Thermopylae spirit as one of the two foundations of the evolution of human culture, the second being the Athenian concept of citizenry. The appreciation of the military virtues of the Spartans and of the heroism at Thermopylae can also be found in the works of the academician and statesman Karl Wilhelm von Humboldt (1767-1835), who considered military training an indispensable part of education.

Thermopylae also appears frequently in German poetry of the same period. The philhellenic poems "Lieder der Griechen" ("Songs of the

Greeks") (6) of Wilhelm Müller are well known. In these, the tradition of Thermopylae is closely connected with the efforts of the Greeks to free themselves from the Ottoman Turks. In a vision, Leonidas visits Alexandros Ypsilantes in his Austrian prison cell and urges him to continue the fight.

The Third Reich also attached great importance to Thermopylae (7). Alfred Rosenberg (1893-1945) was an influential member of the Nazi party and its chief racial theorist. In his book "Der Mythus des zwanzigsten Jahrhunderts" (1925-30), "The Myth of the 20th Century," he sees the Spartans as the protectors of the purity of the Aryan Race and of its civilization and considers Thermopylae as the battle of Europe against Asian mentality.

In World War II, the example of Thermopylae was not used much by the Germans as they successfully advanced on all fronts. Only when the situation turned difficult did some reference appear. The Battle for Stalingrad was a primary example. The encirclement of General Paulus' 6th Army and its fierce resistance was then likened to the Spartans at Thermopylae, who fell in the line of duty for their ideals (8), while Simonides' famous epigram was published in the press and broadcast on the radio.

In the same year, 1943, with Germany visibly losing the war, an article under the title "Sparta as a Model and a Warning" (Sparta, Vorbild und Mahnung) was published in the serious literary magazine "Die Antike." The German Luftwaffe had organized a suicide unit similar to the kamikaze units of Japan following a request to Hitler by Hanna Reitsch, the famous woman test pilot. The unit, commanded by bomber pilot Werner Baumbach (1917-1953), was part of

the secret bomber wing KG 200 Geheim Geschwader and was named "Leonidas."

During the postwar era, the rapid expansion of the parliamentary democracies in the West and the resulting prosperity enjoyed by their societies discouraged any further reference to ancient heroic principles. Thermopylae was now merely a memory from a distant past that had little relation to the present. During that time, a statue of Leonidas was erected in Sparta, Winsconsin, in the United States. After 1960, the movies of the period began to include scenarios based on antiquity, and the

"The Battle of Thermopylae": A painting by Frank Miller ("300," by Frank Miller). The latter book has already been made into a film titled "300," which has enjoyed tremendous commercial success. (published by ΜΑΜΟΥΘΚΟΜΙΞ, Athens, 1999)

The final moments of the Spartans and the Thespians on Kolonos Hill. They all fell to the last man from the rain of Persian arrows. A little earlier, on the dawn of last day of the Thermopylae battle, all surviving warriors had formed a battle line in the open area - and not in the narrow pass - like men marching to death («ως επί θανάτω έξοδον»). This model vignette is the creation of Grigoris Marmatakis and has been made with 54mm figures from various manufacturers (Andrea Miniatures, Pegaso Models, El Viejo Dragon, Preiser, and Verlinden Productions). The figures have been improved extensively and scratch-built parts have been added, while more detail has been added by sculpting parts from two-part epoxy putty. (photo by Stelios Demiras, magazine Model Expert)

renowned battle was depicted in a number of films, sometimes with pleasing visual results. The film "The 300 Spartans" is from that period (1962).

The story of Thermopylae continued to thrive in literary works. Modern novels, based on the battle, attracted the public's intense interest in the 1990s, indicating a return to heroic ideals in a period of international tumult and insecurity. Such works include "Lo scudo di Talos" ("The Spartan", 1988), written by the Italian archeologist Valerio Massimo Manfredi, and "Gates of Fire" (1998) written by the American novelist Steven Pressfield (9). The latter book will be soon made into a film and will offer a new visual re-enactment of the battle. This novel has also been adopted in the syllabus of reading material of the Annapolis United States Naval Academy, which produces officers for the United States Navy and Marine Corps. This fact reveals that the study of Sparta's contributions in military tactics and in the formation of military principles is

considered important by the Americans. A quick analogy could present the United States of America as a new Sparta fighting to retain its ways of life against the various terrorist threats.

In recent Greek history, the Battle of Thermopylae reappeared just before the outbreak of the 1821 National Revolution against the Turks.

The heroic image of Thermopylae for the Greeks under Turkish occupation has often figured in the literary works published since the end of the 18th century. In an effort to bolster the spirit of revolution among the occupied Greeks, Constantinos Regas had written a poem titled "Patriotic Hymn" (1798) praising the virtues of the Thermopylae warriors.

A major Greek poet from Alexandria, Constantine P. Cavafis (1863-1933), also used the Thermopylae theme in an impressive way. In his work, this historical event is seen in the light of responsibilities and moral duties a man should possess. Cavafy wrote his poem "Thermopylae" during the period

The statue of Leonidas, with spear and shield at the ready, at Thermopylae and, on the base, the inscription «ΜΟΛΩΝ ΛΑΒΕ» ("Come and get them"). (The sculpture is by Vassos Falireas)

from 1900 to 1904 (10), and it is possibly the best and most successful revival of the Thermopylae theme:

> "Let honor be to those in whose life it was set to guard Thermopylae.
> Never moving away from duty;
> Just and equals in all of their acts
> But with sadness and compassion
> Brave once they are rich and when They are poor, again brave
> Coming to aid as much as they can;
> Always speaking the truth
> But without hate for those who lie.
> And even more honor they deserve
> When it's predicted (and many predict)
> That Ephialtes will appear in the end
> And the Medes will finally pass through."

During the World War II clashes in 1940-41 between the Greeks and the Italians and Germans, the Thermopylae theme was again revived for two distinctly different occasions. While the heroic fighting by the Greek army against the Italians took place in the Pindus mountains of Northern Epirus, emphasis of the theme was placed on the heroic aspects of the battle. Later, when the British Expeditionary Force fought the Germans at the Thermopylae site in April 1941, the fighting was again likened to the ancient battle.

A monument, sculptured by Vassos Falireas, was erected in 1955 on the site of the ancient battleground of Thermopylae. On the central pedestal stands a bronze statue of Leonidas armed with spear and shield, with «Μολών Λαβέ» ("Come and get them") inscribed on the base. Two more sculptures flank the sides and portray the two mountains, Mt. Taygetos and Mt. Parnon. There is one additional statue of Leonidas in the city of Sparta, where the common tomb of the warriors is also preserved. Both of the sculptural compositions of Leonidas are based on an ancient sculpture of a warrior thought to represent the Spartan king who, as mentioned earlier, was unearthed by the British School of Archeology in the 1920s.

Many streets and squares throughout Greece have been named after Leonidas and Thermopylae to

This statue of Leonidas in Sparta is based on a contemporary sculpture identified, although not confirmed, as Leonidas. (Paul Catledge: "The Spartans - An Epic History," London, 2003, Pan Books)

honor their memory. The name Leonidas is also often given to many men in Greece. The mention of the moral virtues exhibited at Thermopylae and shown by Leonidas is frequent in contemporary Greek life and it is often associated with external threats faced by Greece at the present time. The Battle of Thermopylae has, with the passing of time, gained an important place in our contemporary world, while the ever-growing importance of those virtuous qualities of old tend to disappear. These virtues were bravery, honor, patriotism, and a disciplined morality that often went as far as self-sacrifice.

Notes

1. See I. Kotoulas: The Peloponnesian War: The Twilight of Classical Greece, Periscopio Publications, Athens 2004 (In the Greek language).
2. See the publication by R. Sabbadini in Miscellanea Ceriani, 1910. pp. 183 and onward.
3. The study written by H.T. Parker "The Cult of Antiquity and the French Revolutionaries," London, 1937, is useful on this issue.
4. For general comments, see Eugène Asse's book "L'Indépendance de la Grèce et les poètes de la Restauration," Paris, 1898. See also the following works: G. de Pons, Othryadas, 1820, J. Barbey, "Aux héros des Thermopyles," 1825, C. Gouverne, "Leonidas aux Thermopyles," 1827, E. Mercoeur, "Le Songe ou les Thermopyles," 1827.
5. The identification of Sparta with armed action is also portrayed in "Der Archipelagus" 271: dann, dann, o ihr Freuden Athens! Ihr Taten in Sparta!
6. There were three collections in total: Lieder der Griechen, 1821, Neue Lieder der Griechen, 1823, and Neueste Lieder der Griechen, 1824.
7. A general article on Sparta from the National-Socialist German viewpoint can be found in I. Loukas' book "National Socialism and Hellenism," Grigoris Publications, Athens, 1991, pp. 178-85.
8. See I. Kotoulas: "Propaganda and ideology in the battle of Stalingrand," "Great Battles" magazine Stalingrad issue no.10, pp 52-63, Periscopio Publications, Athens, 2003 (In the Greek language).
9. These works were translated into Greek, Pressfield's by Editions Livanis, Athens 2002, and Manfredi's by Editions Patakis, Athens 2000. Pressfield was also honored in 2003 by the Spartan authorities for his contribution to the advancement of the ancient history of Laconia.
10. Compare with: L. Politis, A History of Modern Greek Literature, MIET Publications, Athens, 1988 (1978), p. 229.

The later battles at Thermopylae

The battle of Thermopylae between the Persians and the Greeks in 480 BC was one of the most important battles of ancient history. However, in the same area of Thermopylae, other battles were fought in defense of Greece from enemy invasions.

In 279 BC, Greek armies from a number of cities gathered at the Thermopylae pass in order to stop the Gauls from invading southern Greece. The Gauls, however, encroaching from central Europe, arrived at the frontiers of the Balkan peninsula. After pillaging the kingdom of Macedonia, they attempted to advance south through the Thermopylae pass.

It was there that they came face to face with a Greek force of 14,000 hoplites. The majority of this force were Aetolians, but included some Athenians, Megareans, Locrians, Phocians, and Boetians. The command of the Greek army had been entrusted to the Athenian general Callippus, while General Vrennus commanded the Gauls. The word "Vrennus" may denote a name, but it is also possible that it was a title for the leader of the army, as the ancient historians were not familiar with the Celtic language and may have misinterpreted the word. At that time, the area of Thermopylae was different from what it had been at the time of the battle with Xerxes' Persians. The pass was wider, due to silt deposits and rain erosion, and the sea had become deeper so the Greek triremes were able to anchor close to the beach. Initially, the Gallic forces tried to dominate the pass by a frontal attack but were repulsed by the Greeks at the Phocian wall in much the same way as during the previous battle with Xerxes. The Gauls were at a serious disadvantage due to their great number and because they launched massive, disorderly attacks. Their uncoordinated masses in the pass became an easy target for the arrows

A dying Gaul. (Roman sculpture, copy of an original Greek bronze statue from 230 BC, Capitol Museum of Rome)

A 4-drachma coin dating from 193 BC on which the Seleucid King, Antiochus III the Great, is depicted. (Numismatic Collection of the National Archeological Museum of Athens)

German mountain troops at Thermopylae following the 1941 battle and the eviction of the allied defenders from the area.

and spears of the Greeks, who then counterattacked with short, sudden charges. The invaders then tried to bypass the pass by traversing the mountain paths, as Hydarnes' Persians had done, but they were repulsed yet again. Eventually, the Greeks were forced to evacuate the pass using their ships to escape. Vrennus then sent a Gallic force to attack Aetolia and force the Aetolians to desert from the Greek army and return to their territory to save it. He also took part of his army and marched to Delphi to pillage the treasures of the Delphic oracle. However, both of these Gallic forces were defeated, suffering heavy losses. The Gauls that remained were subsequently defeated and evicted from Greece by the Macedonian king, Antigonus Gonatas.

In the summer of 191 BC, the Romans and their allies fought the Syrian King, Antiochus III, at Thermopylae. The Syrian king had an army of 10,000 troops, but by that time he was in a dire situation. Most of his allies had either deserted him or were unwilling to actively assist him. The Romans, on the contrary, had

40,000 troops and enjoyed the support of King Philip V of Macedonia, a former enemy. Commanding the Roman forces were Gabrion and Cato, the famous Roman orator. The latter was suspicious of the influence of Greek culture on his fellow Romans. To stop the Roman advance in the area, Antiochus had built a wall protected by a moat. In addition, three forts, built earlier by the Aetolians, guarded the mountain paths. The Romans, however, managed to subdue one of these forts and to encircle the Syrian king's army. Antiochus III suffered a disastrous defeat and was forced to withdraw to Asia Minor.

When the battle between the Romans and Antiochus was fought, the pass was no longer narrow. The Sperchios River had built up deposits that had drastically changed the morphology of the ground from what it had been at the time of Leonidas' sacrifice. The pass had gradually lost its defensive value. In the surrounding region, however, very important events were to take place. During the Greek Revolution of 1821, the Battle of Alamana occurred, in which Athanasios Diakos followed the example of the Spartans and the Thespians and fought to the end to stop the advance of the Turkish-Albanian forces. In the unfortunate Greek War of 1897, a military camp was constructed at Thermopylae, and during its construction significant archeological remains were discovered. Finally, during Easter 1941, one more battle for Greece's freedom took place at Thermopylae when British, Australian, and New Zealand forces clashed with the German invaders but were forced to retreat due to the superiority of the German forces.

The opposing commanders

Leonidas I

Leonidas was the King of Sparta, the 17th of the Agiad Royal line, one of the sons of King Anaxandridas II of Sparta and his first wife. His elder brother was Dorieus, and his youngest brother Cleombrotus. He succeeded his half brother, Cleomenes I, who had, in turn, succeeded Anaxandridas II. In 488 BC, Cleomenes I died without leaving a male heir for the throne. As Dorieus had been killed in a military expedition in Sicily, Leonidas succeeded to the throne and was married to Cleomenes' daughter, Gorgo, who bore him a son, Pleistarchus, who in turn succeeded his father to the throne following the Battle of Thermopylae. In 480 BC, Leonidas went to Thermopylae with a small force of 300 of his finest soldiers, with their attendant helots and perioikoi. On arrival, he was given command of the Greek army that had assembled to stop Xerxes' crossing through the pass. While at Thermopylae, Leonidas succeeded in reconciling the diverse views prevailing among the different commanders of the forces of competing Greek cities. In contrast to the Spartan admiral, Eurybiades, who had revealed a narrow-minded spirit favoring local differences, Leonidas acted with foresight and tried to strengthen the alliance of the Greek cities, as he believed that this very alliance was the key to facing the Persian threat. His decision to hold the Thermopylae pass, despite the certain death that awaited him, turned Leonidas into an eternal example of faith and devotion to the cause of freedom and the principles of honor. Following his heroic stance, the Greeks had his example to imitate. Leonidas proved that Sparta, despite being behind in the creation of artistic treasures, could pride itself for creating one of the highest achievements of mankind, that of making people free.

Demophilos

Unfortunately, nothing is known about the leader of the Thespians who sacrificed themselves alongside Leonidas' Spartans. He must have been a respected Thespian citizen because command of the force of 700 warriors the Thespians sent to Thermopylae was entrusted to him. It is quite probable that, in the days preceding the final battle, he and his hoplites distinguished themselves in action and this influenced Leonidas' decision to retain them for the defense of the pass. An additional reason that may have led Leonidas to such a decision was the belief that the Thespians, like the Spartans, were considered to be descendants of Hercules.

•••••••

Xerxes I

Xerxes is the Greek form of the Old Persian royal name Xsayiarsa, meaning "Ruler of Men" or king. Xerxes was son of Darius I and Atossa, the daughter of Cyrus the Great. Darius appointed him to the throne by excluding the rightful heir, his elder son Artabazanes. It is believed that Xerxes succeeded to the throne when he was around 35. During the preceding 12 years, he had served his father as ruler of Babylon. On becoming king, his first action was to suppress the revolts in Egypt and Babylon, which had broken out in 486 BC, and to appoint his brother, Achaemenes, governor, or satrap, over Egypt. He succeeded in suppressing the Egyptian revolt with the use of cruel methods and pillaging the Nile delta region and was equally ruthless in punishing the people of Babylon. As soon as these peoples had been suppressed, Xerxes began preparations for his invasion of Greece. In this decision, he was influenced by a number of advisors, with Mardonius instrumental among them. These persuaded him that the invasion

The opposing commanders

would punish the Athenians for their victory at Marathon, and it would ensure that the Ionian provinces would not rise up in a possible new revolt. Thus, Xerxes led his army and commanded it at the Thermopylae battle himself. After his Persian army succeeded in crossing the pass of Thermopylae, Xerxes conquered Boeotia and Attica and burned Athens. The Persian fleet was, however, defeated at the naval Battle of Salamis. So, Xerxes, having lost many ships, decided to retreat into Asia to avoid the risk of being trapped in Greece in case the Greeks destroyed the Hellespont bridges he had built. After Xerxes had departed, the Persian army was defeated at the Battle of Plataea, finally putting an end to Xerxes' invasion. The war against the Greeks continued for many years, continuing even after Xerxes' death, but the Persian king played no further direct part in it. The tactical initiative had passed to the Athenians, who deprived the Persians of their control of the western Asia Minor coastal regions, and, in a later campaign, also undertook an invasion of

Egypt but failed. After his withdrawal from Greece, Xerxes became introverted and busied himself with an ambitious plan of the luxurious construction at Persepolis, the center of his kingdom. He was, however, cajoled by his court conspirators into murdering many members of his family. Finally, in 465 BC, he also became a victim of one such conspiracy. His son, Artaxerxes I, succeeded him to the Persian throne.

• • • • • • •

Hydarnes

Very little is known about Hydarnes, the commander of the elite corps of "Immortals," who, along with this force, undertook the encirclement of the Greek army by following the path indicated by Ephialtes. He doubtless enjoyed the confidence of the Persian monarch, as he had also been entrusted with command of the King's personal bodyguard.

Battle memories

- Leonidas became king of Sparta unexpectedly. He had two elder brothers, and this fact made the thought of him mounting the throne improbable. However, his eldest brother, Cleomenes, died while he was king and had no son to succeed him. His other brother, Dorieus, was killed in Sicily, where he had been sent to fight as the leader of a mercenary force. Thus, the throne descended to Leonidas.

- During the first days of the Thermopylae battle, Xerxes leapt up from his throne three times at the sight of the heavy losses that his army, and especially his "Immortals," were subjected to.

- Ephialtes, the son of Eurydemos, came from Antikyra in the province of Malis. Hoping for a large monetary reward, he revealed the secret path to the Persians. Following the defeat of the Persians and their departure from Greece, he escaped to Thessaly fearing punishment by the Lacedaemonians, who had already offered a reward for his capture. Herodotus writes that Ephialtes later returned to Antikyra, where a Trachinian named Athenades murdered him. His death was probably not connected to his treason, but the Lacedaemonians bestowed honors on Athenades for killing him.

- In addition to Ephialtes, two more men were accused of treason: Onetes, the son of Phanagoras from Carystos, and Korydallos from Antikyra. Herodotus, however, rejects this possibility and claims that Ephialtes was the only man responsible. He supports his argument by stating that it was only Ephialtes who was wanted by the Aphictyony of Delphi with offer of a reward. In his view, the members of the Amphictyony must surely have researched the matter well and collected the correct information before deciding who the actual traitor was.

- According to Herodotus, the Delphic oracle had issued a prediction that stated that when the Persians invaded, Sparta would be destroyed or one of its kings would die. Selecting one of the two oracular options, Leonidas decided to sacrifice himself so that the city could be saved.

- In his morning sacrificial rites on the last day of the battle, the soothsayer, Megistias from Acarnania, divined that the defenders of Thermopylae would die. Leonidas then ordered him to leave with the rest of the army, but he refused to do so and just allowed his only son to leave.

- The Lacedaemonians brought Leonidas' bones to Sparta in 440 BC. The tomb they built had a stele inscribed with the names of all 300 warriors.

- A Spartan warrior, Dieneces, distinguished himself in the battle. Before the battle, a Trachinian said that the Persian archers were so many that their arrows would hide the sky. Dieneces' answer to this was "all the better, as we will then fight in the shade."

- The Spartan brothers Alpheus and Maron, sons of Orsiphantus, and the Thespian warrior Dithyrambos, the son of Armatides, were also among those who distinguished themselves during the battle.

- To honor all the Peloponnesian defenders of the pass, the following epigram was inscribed: "Here once fought 4,000 Peloponnesians against 3,000,000 Persians."

A special epigram was also composed to honor the Thespians: "These men once lived on the foothills of Mt. Helicon. The wide plain of Thespian country is proud of their courage."

Another epigram was dedicated to the Opuntian Locrians, who fell during the first two days of the battle. It reads: "The metropolis of Lokroi misses those who died defending Greece against the Medes."

Lesser-known details

The most famous epigram, by Simonides of Ceos, was inscribed on the tomb of the Spartans:

"Oh stranger, go tell the Lacedaemonians that we lie buried here obedient to their orders."

The Spartans also dedicated a special epigram to the soothsayer Megistias, who had refused to abandon Leonidas, despite knowing the outcome was certain death.

● On the day of the battle, two of the 300 Spartans, Eurytus and Aristodemus, had fallen ill at Alpenoi. Leonidas had allowed them to leave with the rest of the army as they were in no condition to fight. Eurytus, however, refused to leave and ordered his helot escort to help him into his armor and to hand him his weapons and to take him to Thermopylae. He died there alongside his fellow hoplites. According to a different theory, these two men were messengers and were away from the battleground at the time delivering a message. Eurytus hastened his return in order to take part in the battle, while Aristodemus delayed his return in order to avoid it. Whatever the truth, upon his return to Sparta, Aristodemus was tried for cowardice but was acquitted. Despite his acquittal, the Spartans held him in contempt. To restore

his honor, Aristodemus showed extreme bravery in the later Battle of Plataea.

● According to Herodotus, one more Spartan avoided the battle. He was the messenger, Pantites, who was away in Thessaly on duty. When he returned to Sparta he also faced the contempt of his fellow citizens and, in his grief, he committed suicide.

● Mythology often influenced the behavior of both Greeks and Persians, as the majority of people at that time were devout religious believers in its teachings. It may thus be probable that Leonidas decided to share glory with the Thespians in

belief of the myth that both he and the Thespians descended from the hero Hercules. Herodotus writes that Xerxes succeeded in obtaining the neutrality of the Argives because the Persian envoys had told them that, according to mythology, both shared a common ancestry. The Argives worshipped Perseus as a hero of their city, and he was considered the father of Perses, the mythical original ancestor of the Persians.

Bibliography

1. Aeschylus: THE PERSIANS.
2. Herodotus: THE HISTORIES.
3. Plutarch: MORALIA (Essays).
4. Herman Bengtson: GRIECHISCHE GESCHICHTE, Verlag C. H. Beck, Munich, 1994.
5. J.B. Bury & R. Meiggs: A HISTORY OF ANCIENT GREECE, Kardamitsas Publications, Athens, 1992 (In the Greek language).
6. N.G.L. Hammond: A HISTORY OF GREECE TO 322 BC, Oxford University Press, Oxford, 1986.
7. A HISTORY OF THE GREEK NATION, Ekdotiki Athinon Publication, Athens, 1982 (In the Greek language).
8. A HISTORY OF ANCIENT GREECE by Panayiotis Kannelopoulos, D. Gialelis Publications, Athens, 1982 (In the Greek language).
10. Claude Mossé & Annie Schnapp-Gourbeillon: A HISTORY OF ANCIENT GREECE, Papadimas Publications, Athens, 2000 (In the Greek language).
11. Georg Steinhauer: WAR IN ANCIENT GREECE, Papadimas Publications, Athens, 2000 (In the Greek language).
12. J.W. Baird; THE MYTHOLOGICAL WORLD OF NAZI WAR PROPAGANDA 1939-1945, University of Minnesota Press, Minneapolis, 1974.
13. E.M. Butler: THE TYRANNY OF GREECE OVER GERMANY, Cambridge University Press, 1958 (1933).
14. P. Cartledge: THE SPARTANS; AN EPIC HISTORY, Pan Books, London, 2003.
15. M.I. Finley: THE MYTH OF SPARTA, The Listener, August 2, 1962m pp. 171-3.
16. S.L. Hormouzios (ed.): SALUTE TO GREECE: AN ANTHOLOGY OF CARTOONS PUBLISHED IN THE BRITISH PRESS, London, 1991 (1942).
17. R. Jenkyns: THE VICTORIANS AND ANCIENT GREECE, Oxford, 1980.
18. Christos Kardaras: THE LACEDAEMONIANS: A POLITICAL, SOCIAL, STATE POLICY, AND RELIGIOUS HISTORY OF ANCIENT SPARTA, Athens, 1979 (In the Greek language).
19. I. Kotoulas: PROPAGANDA AND IDEOLOGY IN THE BATTLE OF STALINGARD, "Great Battles" magazine Stalingrad issue no.10, pp 52-63, Periscopio Publications, Athens, 2003 (In the Greek language).
20. I. Kotoulas: PHILOLOGY AND POLITICS: THE IMAGE OF SPARTA IN THE 19TH AND 20TH CENTURIES, Address to the 2nd Congress of the Association of Laconic Studies, Sparta, (29th - 30th October 2004).
21. I. Loukas: NATIONAL SOCIALISM AND HELLENISM, Grigoris Publications, Athens, 1991 (In the Greek language).
22. E. Rawson: THE SPARTAN TRADITION IN EUROPEAN THOUGHT, Oxford University Press, Oxford, 1969.
23. E.N. Tigerstedt: THE LEGEND OF SPARTA IN CLASSICAL ANTIQUITY, 3 Volumes, Stockholm, Uppsala and Göteborg, 1965-1978.
24. F.M. Turner: THE GREEK HERITAGE IN VICTORIAN BRITAIN, New Haven and London, 1981.

Introductory Note

A limited glossary has been provided below that covers most of the terms that may be unfamiliar to readers. It is in alphabetical order for ease of use.

GLOSSARY

Aegina: Aegina is the island in the bay opposite Athens. According to Herodotus, it was a colony of Epidaurus, to which state it was originally subject. Its placement between Attica and the Peloponnesus made it a center of trade even earlier, and its earliest inhabitants came from Asia Minor. Minoan ceramics have been found in contexts of c. 2000 BC. The discovery on the island of a number of gold ornaments belonging to the latest period of Mycenaean art suggests the inference that the Mycenaean culture held its own in Aegina for some generations after the Dorian conquest of Argos and Lacedaemon. It is probable that the island was not doricized before the 9th century BC.

akinakes: The characteristic Persian sidearm was the akinakes, which was short in length but could be used for both cut and thrust. It is of Scythian origin, adopted by both the Medes and Persians from at least the 7th century until the 2nd century BC. The sword had a short, straight, double-edged iron blade, 34-45 cm (14-18") in length.

amphora: An amphora (plural: amphorae or amphoras) is a type of ceramic vase with two handles and a long neck narrower than the body that was mainly used for wine, olive oil, and other liquids.

amrtaka: Amrtaka is believed to be the ancient Iranian name of the "Immortals."

Anopaia: The path leading through the mountains to Thermopylae through which Ephialtes led the Persians to the Greeks from the rear. Some researchers say that upon learning of an alternate pass through the mountains at Anopaia to the west, Leonidas, still in command of the Greek forces, deployed a force of 1,000 Phocian hoplites to defend that pass.

Bonapartists: In French political history, the Bonapartists were monarchists who desired a French Empire under the House of Bonaparte, the Corsican family of Napoleon Bonaparte (Napoleon I of France) and his nephew Louis (Napoleon III of France).

crest: The plume of a helmet.

crest holder: The iron part supporting the plume of a helmet.

cuirass: Body armor that protects the torso of the wearer above the waist or hips. Originally it was a thick leather garment covering the body from neck to waist. The Ancient Greeks had a formed leather cuirass, a type of anatomical breastplate that was first achieved from hot, wet-formed leather. In later years, the same form was known as the bronze cuirass. Although the bronze helmet was developed at a fairly early age, bronze was not conceived as body armor for some years later.

curved slashing sword: A short, curved sword using for cutting opponents. Synonym for kopis.

decarch: The commander over 10 people. (decarchy, n. rule by or ruling body of 10 persons, or a military section or platoon of 10 men).

Dokana cult: The Dokana cult was the worship of the hearth and comes down from antiquity from Indo-European times. The hearth was the center of the house cult and of the piety of daily life. Thus, the hearth was sacred, and the daily meal was sacred. The sanctity of the meal found expression in the rites that accompanied it. The "dokana" are the beams of a house built of sun-dried bricks. The sacrifices brought to them are meals, theoxenia, which occur particularly in the house cult. They are especially connected with the Spartan kings, who took them with them when taking the field. The beams appeared as decoration on Spartan shields.

Doriskos: An ancient city 5 km southwest of today's town of Feres.

Dumouriez: Charles François Dumouriez (January 25, 1739 – March 14, 1823) was a French general of the French Revolutionary Wars; he shared the victory at Valmy with General Kellermann and later deserted the Revolutionary Army.

Elamites: The Elamites called their country Haltamti (in later Elamite, Atamti), which the neighboring Akkadians rendered as Elam. Elam means "highland." Additionally, the Haltamti are known as Elam in the Hebrew Old Testament, where they are called the offspring of Elam, eldest son of Shem (see Elam in the Bible). They lived in Elam, one of the oldest recorded civilizations. Elam was centered in the far west and southwest of modern-day Iran (Ilam Province and the lowlands of Khuzestan) and parts of southern Iraq. It lasted from around 2700 BC to 539 BC. It was preceded by what is known as the Proto-Elamite period, which began around 3200 BC when Susa (later capital of Elam) began to be influenced by the cultures of the Iranian plateau to the east.

greaves: The protecting shields for the shins of the legs worn by ancient warriors.

Hellenes: The Greeks by another name of Greek derivation. The word derives from "Hellas," Greece, in Greek.

Hellenism: As used in the text: The Greek world of the period, including all the areas and cities where Greeks (Hellenes) lived.

helots: A class of Spartan people. The Spartans were divided into two broad categories: the residents of the pre-Doric towns, who enjoyed a free but dependent status as "Perioikoi," and the peasants, who enjoyed a far more restricted status as "helots." The "helots," or rural population, had a significantly worse status. These "helots" were tied to the land and were officially the property of the Lacedaemonian government. As a result of at least one and possibly more revolts, they were regarded with increasing suspicion and subjected to increasingly harsher laws. In fact, the Lacedaemonian government regularly declared war on the helots to enable quick retribution against any "unruly" helot without the tedious business of a trial. This unique situation led many contemporary ancient commentators to remark on the "exceptional" harshness of the Spartan system.

hoplite: A heavily armed foot soldier in Greek armies, typically of the citizen class.

kerkouroi: Auxiliary ships for the transport of grain (and other food) and soldiers, also known as "aphracts."

Kerkyra: Kerkyra or Corcyra or Corfu (Greek: Κέρκυρα, Kérkyra, Ancient Greek Κέρκυρα or Κόρκυρα, Latin: Corcyra, Italian Corfù) is a Greek island in the Ionian Sea. It lies off the coast of Albania, from which it is separated by straits varying in breadth from 3 to 23 km (2 to 15 mi), including one near Butrint and a longer one west of Thesprotia. The island is part of the Corfu Prefecture. The principal town of the island is also named Corfu, or Kerkyra in Greek. The island is steeped in history and it is perennially connected to the history of Greece starting from Greek mythology.

Kerkyreans: The people of the island of Kerkyra.

KG 200 Geheim Geschwader: KG 200 Geheim Geschwader was the Luftwaffe Leonidas Squadron under the command of Lieutenant Colonel Heiner Lang, and it flew "self-sacrifice missions" ("Selbstopfereinsatz") against Soviet held bridges over the Oder River from 17 April until 20 April 1945 during the Battle for Berlin.

Kissians: The Kissians were a part of the Persian Army and served with equipment in other respects like that of the Persians, but instead of the usual felt caps they wore fillets.

koinon: The community federation (koinon) of Thessaly. The koinon was an administrative division of the area belonging to a town.

Lacedaemon: The river plain surrounding Sparta itself, often used synonymously for the city or the Spartan state. The initial letter Λ (lambda), the Greek "L", was the shield blazon of the Spartan soldier.

Laconians: The inhabitants of the southeastern section of the Peloponnesus, named Laconia, of which Sparta was the chief city.

Markos Botsaris: Markos Botsaris (Greek Μάρκος Μπότσαρης, Albanian Marko Boçari, c. 1788 - 21 August 1823) was a Greek leader who played an important role in the Greek War of Independence of 1821.

Medes: A major Persian race, but the word is often used by Greek writers to denote all Persians regardless of whether they were Medes or Persians or other ethnicities under Persian rule.

Median: Adjective from Mede: pertaining to the Medes.

Moralia: A large part of Plutarch's surviving essay work is collected under the title of the Moralia (loosely translated as Customs and Mores). It is an eclectic collection of 78 essays and transcribed speeches.

Mt. Parnon: Parnon or Malevo is a mountain ridge on the east of the Laconian plain. Its height is 1,940 m. It is visible from Athens above the top of the Argive mountains. The Parnon range separates Laconia from Arcadia and is predominantly limestone. This mountain is home to the fifth deepest cave in Greece, the Peleta Sinkhole, and the impressive vertical cave Propantes.

numismatic: Adjective: pertaining to coins.

Peloponnesus: The large southern peninsula of mainland Greece, home to Laconia and other regions and connected to central Greece by the isthmus of Corinth. Its inhabitants are known as the Peloponnesians.

pentaconter (penteconter): A Greek vessel with 50 oars and manned by 50 oarsmen.

perioikoi: The periokoi or "dwellers around" were free men of Sparta, mainly farmers and merchants, who lacked the full citizenship of the Spartans. They lived in perhaps 80 or 100 towns and villages, which were called poleis (the plural of polis), in the less fertile land of the hills and coasts. They may have been part of a conquered people, but unlike the helots, they kept their freedom. Perhaps they were conquered earlier; perhaps the helot serfs were periokoi who rebelled. The singular of perioikoi is perioikos. The perioikoi had their own laws and customs, could pursue any profession or trade they liked and had their own local officials and dignitaries. They were restricted only with regard to foreign and military policy, being subject to the government of the entire territory or city-state, Lacedaemon, which was run by Spartans. They were also required to provide troops for the Lacedaemonian army and to support Sparta in time of war. Because the Spartan citizens were themselves prohibited by their laws from engaging in any profession except that of arms, the Perioikoi were the professionals, merchants, and craftsmen of Lacedaemon, and they were not prohibited from hoarding gold and silver. In short, they had a monopoly on all lucrative businesses and professions. They were the only people allowed to travel to other cities, which the Spartans were not, unless given permission. The name derives from (περί / peri, "around" and οἶκος / oikos, "dwelling, house").

phalanx: A tight formation of hoplites, typically eight ranks or more deep, in a line of battle, very effective in battle and difficult to oppose.

Philhellenic Movement: The movement in support of the Greek uprising of 1821 against the Turks. The Philhellenes helped the Greeks in various ways in their war of Independence after 1821 and until Greece was freed from the Turkish yoke.

Phleiasians: The people of Phleious, an ancient city in the Argolid area of Peloponnesus, not far from Nemea.

Preliminary councilors: The preliminary councilors were elderly officials in a city who decided in council on important matters such as war expeditions and military strategy and important political or economic changes. In Athens, this "board of elders" («ἀρχήν τινα πρεσβυτέρων ἀνδρῶν») were "to be preliminary councilors" («προβουλεύσουσιν») to Athens. Aristotle, in his work on politics, has an interesting and relevant discussion of councils (βουλαί) and boards of preliminary councilors (Aristotle, Politics: 1299b).

probouloi: The preliminary councilors.

sauroter: The base of a spear, usually in the form of a round sphere or spear head. This was a long slender spike, 30-40 centimeters in length, usually with a square cross-section, made of cast bronze. It is believed to have served several functions. Firstly, it was used to stand the spear on the ground when it was not being used, and for this reason the Greeks called it a sauroter, which literally means "lizard killer." Secondly, the butt-spike may have served as a secondary weapon if the spearhead broke off, an event that was reasonably common in the heat of battle, as Herodotus and Thucydides attest. Thirdly, it was supposedly used by the men standing behind those at the front, who were doing the actual fighting, to finish off any fallen enemy that the phalanx walked over as they rolled forward.

slashing sword: A short sword, usually uncurved, used to cut down opponents; synonym to the Greek "kopis" for a sword of this type.

soft cap: A soft cap for the head, called "pilos" by the Greeks.

sparabara: A Persian shield bearer.

St. Marcellin: St. Marcellin is a town in the French region of Isère. The town was temporarily renamed Thermopyles in honor of the battle.

stele: A stele (from Greek: στήλη, stele, IPA: [stili]; plural: stelae, στῆλαι, stelai, IPA: [stilae]; also found: Latinised singular stela and Anglicised plural steles) is a stone or wooden slab, generally taller than it is wide, erected for funerary or commemorative purposes, most usually decorated with the names and titles of the deceased or living, inscribed, carved in relief (bas-relief, sunken-relief, high-relief, etc.), or painted onto the slab.

Strymon: The Strymon River flowed into the Aegean Sea between the Chalcidice Peninsula and the island of Thasos.

tagoi: Thessalian term for the local leaders of the community federation (koinon) of Thessaly.

taka: A type of shield used by Persian warriors, usually horsemen on Median horses, which originated from the crescent-shaped Scythian "taka" shield of similar design.

takabara: A Persian taka shield bearer.

Taygetos: Taygetus or Taygetos (Greek: Ταΰγετος), also Taigetos, is a mountain range of the Peloponnesus, Southern Greece, extending about 65 mi (100 km) north from the southern end of Cape Matapan in the Mani Peninsula. It rises to about 7,900 ft (2,410 m) at Mt. Hagios Ilias (Mt. St. Elias or Prophitis Elias). The mountain range includes the prefectures of Arcadia, Laconia, and Messenia.

Tempe: Also known as Tempi, the narrow ravine in the Peneios river valley.

Thermopylae: The word means "Hot Gates;" a pass between the mountains and the sea connecting central with northern Greece where the battle of Thermopylae was fought.

Thermopyles: Old temporary name of St. Marcellin, a town in the French region of Isère.

triconter: A Triconter is a Greek vessel with 30 oars and manned by 30 oarsmen.

Trireme: Trireme (Greek Τριήρεις pl.,Τριήρης sing.) refers to a class of warships used by ancient Greeks and Romans. In English, no differentiation is made between the Greek "trieres" and the Latin "triremes." This is sometimes a source of confusion, as in other languages these terms refer to different styles of ships. The early type had three rows of oars on each side, manned with one man per oar. They originated with the Phoenicians and are best known from the fleets of Ancient Greece.

Μολών Λαβέ: (in Greek) the famous Laconic dictum of Leonidas which means "Come and get them."

Nikos Th. Tselepides